A HISTORICAL READER

Japanese-American
Internment

nextext

Printed in the United States of America
ISBN 0-618-00365-7

1 2 3 4 5 6 7 — QKT — 06 05 04 03 02 01 00

Table of Contents

PART V: REMEMBRANCE AND REDRESS

*Throughout the reader, vocabulary words appear in boldface
type and are footnoted. Specialized or technical words and phrases
appear in lightface type and are footnoted.*

Pearl Harbor and Anti-Japanese Bias

from

Eagle Against the Sun

BY RONALD SPECTOR

Throughout the 1930s, Japan aggressively expanded her power in the Pacific, coming more and more into conflict with the United States, which opposed Japan's efforts to establish military and economic control of Asia. The Japanese invasion of China in 1937 put the two countries on the path to war. Deciding that war was unavoidable, the Japanese struck first, attacking the U.S. fleet stationed at Pearl Harbor in Hawaii on December 7, 1941. This surprise attack brought the United States into World War II. The following selection is the historian Ronald Spector's account of the attack on Pearl Harbor.

They came in from the north over the blue-green hills of Kahuku Point on Oahu. In steady waves, 181 Japanese fighters, dive-bombers, and torpedo planes—the most modern, highly trained and deadly naval air force in the world—roared across the island toward their targets. It was 7:40 A.M., the morning of December 7, 1941.

The Japanese planes were **deployed**[1] in four groups; and headed south toward the Pacific Fleet base at Pearl Harbor and the nearby air bases at Ewa, Hickam Field, and Kaneohe. Inside the crowded anchorage of Pearl Harbor were ninety-six ships of the Pacific Fleet under Admiral Husband E. Kimmel.

The fleet had been in Hawaii since May 1940, acting as a **putative**[2] deterrent to Japanese aggression against British or Dutch possessions in Southeast Asia. Admiral James O. Richardson, who then commanded the Pacific Fleet, thought this was a harebrained idea. He pointed out that in the event of war, the fleet would have to return to the U.S. West Coast anyway. Only by doing so could its crews attain full war strength. The logistical, repair, and training facilities at Pearl Harbor were inferior to those on the West Coast, and prolonged absence from their families in the western states had affected the morale of his men adversely. As for the Japanese, they undoubtedly knew about the unreadiness of the fleet and were unlikely to be deterred by its presence. Richardson was so vociferous in his objections that he was relieved of command at the end of one year and replaced by Admiral Kimmel. The ships remained at Pearl Harbor.

On this particular Sunday morning, all of the battleships of the Pacific Fleet except *Colorado*—which was in dry dock on the West Coast—were at Pearl Harbor. The carriers *Lexington* and *Enterprise*, with their escorting cruisers and destroyers, were at sea: they were delivering aircraft to Wake and Midway Islands. On the airfields near Pearl Harbor, almost four hundred army,

---

[1] **deployed**—spread out on an extended front.

[2] **putative**—assumed; commonly accepted.

navy, and Marine Corps planes were parked: wing-tip to wing-tip—as protection against **sabotage**.[3]

Although Japanese-American relations had been in crisis for several months, no special measures had been taken to prepare for the outbreak of hostilities. Since June 1940 Hawaii had had three major alerts and numerous air-raid and anti-submarine drills. At least as far back as 1936, American war plans had discussed the possibility of a surprise air raid against Pearl Harbor. In March 1941 an army aviator, Major General Frederick L. Martin, and a naval airman, Rear Admiral Patrick N. L. Bellinger, had completed a report on the defense of Hawaii. It specifically pointed out that a surprise attack from the air was "the most likely and dangerous form of attack" against the fleet base on Oahu. Another report— by the Hawaiian air force staff in August 1941—even **conjectured**[4] that the Japanese might employ up to six carriers in such an attack, and that it would probably be delivered in the early morning. Yet in Hawaii no one, as of December 1941, actually believed it could happen. Hawaii was the strongest American base in the Pacific. Army Chief of Staff General George C. Marshall described it to President Roosevelt in May 1941 as

> ". . . the strongest fortress in the world. . . . Enemy carriers, naval escorts and transports will begin to come under air attack at a distance of approximately 750 miles. This attack will increase in intensity until within 200 miles of the objective, the enemy forces will be subject to all types of bombardment closely supported by our most modern pursuit. . . . An invader would face more than 35,000 troops backed by coast defense guns and anti-aircraft artillery."

---

[3] **sabotage**—actions carried out by a civilian or enemy agent designed to hinder a nation's war effort.

[4] **conjectured**—hypothesized, speculated.

However frequently army and navy leaders discussed the possibility of a Japanese attack, in the final analysis it appeared unlikely, almost fantastic.

The feeling that Hawaii was probably immune from attack was reinforced during the autumn of 1941 by constant intelligence reports, news, and rumors concerning Japanese preparations to move against British and Dutch possessions in Southeast Asia and against the Philippines. Few believed that Japan could or would undertake a simultaneous attack against Pearl Harbor. Besides, as Admiral Richardson had bluntly pointed out, there was no need for them to do so. The Pacific Fleet, although **formidable**[5] on paper, was in no shape to contest Japanese moves in the western Pacific. Recalled Captain Vincent R. Murphy, Admiral Kimmel's assistant war plans officer,

> I thought it would be utterly stupid for the Japanese to attack the United States at Pearl Harbor. We could not have materially affected their control of the waters they wanted to control whether or not the battleships were sunk at Pearl Harbor. . . . I did not believe we could move the United States Fleet to the Western Pacific until such time as the material condition of the ships was improved, especially with regard to anti-aircraft and until such time as the Pacific Fleet was materially reinforced.

Admiral Kimmel and Lieutenant General Walter C. Short, commanding general of the Hawaiian Department, thus felt justified in devoting most of their efforts to training; but planes or ships used for training could not at the same time be used for scouting enemy raiders—or held on alert to repel an attack.

---

[5] **formidable**—causing fear or dread.

On the morning of the seventh, the only scouting planes in the air were a few Catalina Flying Boats on routine antisubmarine patrol to the west of Oahu. None of the dozens of army and navy fighters were on alert, and the army's antiaircraft gunners had not been issued live ammunition.

A radar warning system had been set up in August, but it was still operating on a part-time basis. The Signal Corps, which was responsible for training, was reluctant to relinquish control of this system to the Army Air Corps, which was responsible for full-time operations. The part-time schedule which had been arranged called for the radar sets to operate between 4:00 and 7:00 A.M. On this particular morning, however, the radar station at Opana, near Kahuku Point, had not closed down exactly as scheduled and, at 7:02 A.M., the operator detected the attacking Japanese planes about 137 miles north of Oahu. He promptly telephoned the Army Aircraft Warning Service Information Center at Oahu. The duty officer, Lieutenant Kermit Tyler, believed that the aircraft picked up on the Opana radar were a flight of B-17s due to arrive from the mainland—he told the radar operator not to "worry about it."

His mistake was understandable; the information center had no liaison personnel from the navy, Marine Corps, or Army Bomber Command regularly assigned to it. That morning, Tyler and a switchboard operator were the only people in the center. Lieutenant Tyler was a fighter pilot with no previous experience as a controller or with an air-warning system.

At the Harbor Control Post in the operations office of the Fourteenth Naval District, Navy Lieutenant Harold Kaminski faced a somewhat similar problem. At 6:53 A.M., he had received a message from the USS *Ward*, the duty destroyer patrolling off the entrance to Pearl Harbor. The *Ward* had attacked a submarine operating in an area where no submarine had any business to be. Like Lieutenant Tyler, Kaminski was alone with a single telephone operator in his command post. Moreover, he had standing orders to contact over half-a-dozen other command posts and headquarters by telephone in the event of trouble.

Shortly before 7:00 A.M., Kaminski started dialing. He reached the chief of staff, who requested confirmation from the *Ward* and referred the matter to Admiral Kimmel and to Admiral C. C. Bloch, Commandant of the Fourteenth Naval District. Bloch, like Kimmel, decided to wait for confirmation from the *Ward*.

Twelve thousand feet above Oahu, Commander Fuchida Mitsuo stared down at the American battleships moored together in groups of two off Ford Island. "I had seen all German warships assembled in Kiel harbor," he later recalled. "I have also seen the French battleships in Brest. And finally, I have seen our own warships assembled for review before the Emperor, but I have never seen ships, even in the deepest peace, anchored at a distance less than 500 to 1,000 yards from each other. . . . this picture down there was hard to comprehend." At 7:53 Fuchida radioed back to the waiting Japanese task force: "Tora, Tora, Tora"—the code word indicating that surprise had been achieved.

The Japanese dive-bombers and fighters peeled off to attack the air bases, while the torpedo planes, along with dive-bombers and high-level bombers, concentrated on the battleships. Aboard the battleship *West Virginia*, Ensign Roland Brooks, the officer of the deck, mistook the first bomb blast for an internal explosion aboard one of the neighboring ships and instantly gave the order "Away Fire and Rescue Party!" Of all the mistakes on that day, this one alone had fortunate consequences, for Ensign Brooks's alarm started the *West Virginia's* crew running for their stations before the first bombs and torpedoes hit the ship. Although severely damaged, the *West Virginia* suffered relatively few casualties. Hit below the water-line, she avoided capsizing by skillful damage control, and settled right side up on the shallow bottom.

Other ships were not so lucky. The battleship *Arizona* was buried under a rain of bombs, one of which penetrated the forecastle[6] and detonated the forward magazine.[7] More than 80 percent of her crew of over 1,500 men were killed or drowned. The *Oklahoma* was hit by three torpedoes almost simultaneously and rapidly capsized, taking with her over 400 of her crew. The *California,* which had her watertight doors "unbuttoned," for an anticipated inspection, was hit by two torpedoes at the beginning of the attack. "Her bulkheads were so leaky the water entering the great gash [made by these hits] could not be isolated."

In almost all ships, many key officers were ashore for the weekend. In the incredible noise and confusion, the flames of burning oil, and the dull crash of bombs, it was the junior officers, young reserve lieutenants and ensigns, many of them only a few months out of college or the naval academy, who carried most of the burden of command. Ensign J. K. Taussig, a "Navy brat," got the *Nevada* under way in forty-five minutes—a task which normally required two and one-half hours and the assistance of four tugboats. Commanded by Lieutenant Commander Francis J. Thomas, a middle-aged reservist, her antiaircraft guns directed by Ensign Taussig and a second ensign, the *Nevada* steamed **majestically**[8] down the channel and later beached herself near the southern end of Ford Island.

While the Pacific Fleet anchorage was under attack, other Japanese planes bombed and strafed the nearby navy, army, and Marine Corps air bases. Three squadrons

---

[6] forecastle—forward part of a ship's upper deck.

[7] magazine—place where explosives are stored.

[8] **majestically**—with great splendor or glory.

of Catalina Flying Boats from the navy seaplane base at Kaneohe Bay were almost totally destroyed in two successive waves of Japanese dive-bombing attacks. At the principal Army Air Corps fields—Bellows, Wheeler, and Hickam—the closely parked planes would have required a minimum of four hours to be ready for take-off. Within a few minutes, fighters and dive-bombers had knocked out most of the army planes and severely damaged the hangar facilities. The Marine Corps air station at Ewa suffered the same fate. All but two of the dozen Wildcat fighters were destroyed, and Japanese fighters roamed the area freely—shooting up barracks, hangars, and other targets of opportunity.

When the attacks were at their height, the twelve B-17s from the mainland which Lieutenant Tyler had thought Opana was tracking on its radar appeared over Hickam Field. To save weight on the long flight, the big bombers carried no ammunition and their guns were not mounted. Low on fuel, sniped at by Japanese fighters and by nervous American antiaircraft gunners, the B-17 pilots nevertheless managed to land their planes on the wreckage-strewn airfield.

There was a short lull in the battle around eight-thirty, as the first wave of Japanese attackers departed. The defenders took advantage of this brief respite to improvise additional defenses. When the second wave—eighty dive-bombers, fifty-four high-level bombers, and thirty-six fighters—arrived around nine, they were given a hot reception. Six fighters and fourteen dive-bombers of this second group of attackers were lost to antiaircraft fire—more than double the number shot down in the initial onslaught.

The second attack concentrated on the least-damaged ships. The battleship *Pennsylvania*, which was in dry dock, was hit by a bomb which caused minor damage. But two destroyers in the same dock, *Cassin* and *Downes*, were almost totally destroyed. In a nearby floating dock, the destroyer *Shaw's* bow was blown off by a bomb.

By ten o'clock the second wave of attackers had departed, leaving behind six battleships sunk or sinking; two other battleships, three destroyers, and three cruisers damaged. Almost 3,600 men had been killed or wounded. Columns of black smoke, hundreds of feet high, hung over the fleet anchorage. Burning oil covered parts of the harbor as salvage teams worked frantically to free men still trapped in the hulls of sunken ships.

At the airfields, work crews fought fires and struggled to clear away enough of the wreckage to permit takeoffs and landings. One hundred eighty planes had been destroyed and 128 others damaged. At Ewa Marine Air Station and the naval air station at Kaneohe, not a single plane was in condition to fly. Late in the morning a handful of army and navy planes flew off from Hickam field to look for the Japanese task force, which had long since safely withdrawn to the north.

In Washington that afternoon, President Franklin D. Roosevelt met with his military advisors amid reports of Japanese attacks on Guam, Wake, and Hong Kong, as well as against Singapore and other parts of Southeast Asia. Present at the meeting were Secretary of State Cordell Hull, Navy Secretary Frank Knox, Secretary of War Henry L. Stimson, and the two military service chiefs. The president read them a draft message to Congress asking for a declaration of war against Japan.

Around noon the next day, millions of Americans gathered by their radios to listen to the president's six-minute address to the Congress: "Yesterday, December 7, 1941, a date which will live in **infamy** [9] the United States was suddenly and deliberately attacked by naval and air forces of the Empire of Japan." Less than an hour

[9] **infamy**—evil reputation brought about by criminal or brutal acts.

later Congress, with one dissenting vote, approved the declaration of war against Japan.

In Tokyo, the Imperial Rescript announcing the beginning of hostilities was read over the radio by the prime minister, General Tojo Hideki. Then came a Japanese martial song, "Umi Yukaba." It included the lines:

Across the sea, corpses in the water
Across the mountain, corpses in the field.

It was an appropriate overture to the bloody forty-four month war which had now begun.

QUESTIONS TO CONSIDER

1. Why were military personnel lax about fortifying Pearl Harbor against an attack?

2. Why did the junior officers have to carry the burden of command during the surprise strike?

3. In hindsight, do you think the heavy casualties of Pearl Harbor could have been avoided? Why or why not?

Request for a Declaration of War

BY PRESIDENT FRANKLIN D. ROOSEVELT

The day after the attack on Pearl Harbor, President Roosevelt went before a special session of the U.S. Congress to ask for a declaration of war. Immediately after his speech, Congress declared war on Japan with only one dissenting vote. Three days later, war was also declared on Germany and Italy. Roosevelt's speech, which is reproduced below, includes the famous phrase: "a date which will live in infamy."

Yesterday, December 7, 1941—a date which will live in infamy—the United States of America was suddenly and deliberately attacked by naval and air forces of the Empire of Japan.

The United States was at peace with that nation, and, at the **solicitation**[1] of Japan, was still in conversation with its government and its emperor looking toward the maintenance of peace in the Pacific. Indeed, one

---

[1] **solicitation**—application, petition, request.

hour after Japanese air squadrons had commenced bombing in Oahu, the Japanese ambassador to the United States and his colleague delivered to the secretary of state a formal reply to a recent American message. While this reply stated that it seemed useless to continue the existing diplomatic negotiations, it contained no threat or hint of war or armed attack.

It will be recorded that the distance of Hawaii from Japan makes it obvious that the attack was deliberately planned many days or even weeks ago. During the intervening time the Japanese government has deliberately sought to deceive the United States by false statements and expressions of hope for continued peace.

The attack yesterday on the Hawaiian Islands has caused severe damage to American naval and military forces. Very many American lives have been lost. In addition, American ships have been reported torpedoed on the high seas between San Francisco and Honolulu.

Yesterday the Japanese government also launched an attack against Malaya.

Last night Japanese forces attacked Hong Kong.

Last night Japanese forces attacked Guam.

Last night Japanese forces attacked the Philippine Islands.

Last night the Japanese attacked Wake Island.

This morning the Japanese attacked Midway Island.

Japan has, therefore, undertaken a surprise offensive extending throughout the Pacific area. The facts of yesterday speak for themselves. The people of the United States have already formed their opinions and well understand the implications to the very life and safety of our nation.

As commander in chief of the Army and Navy I have directed that all measures be taken for our defense.

Always will we remember the character of the onslaught against us. No matter how long it may take us to overcome this **premeditated**[2] invasion, the American people, in their **righteous**[3] might, will win through to absolute victory. I believe I interpret the will of the Congress and of the people when I assert that we will not only defend ourselves to the uttermost but will make very certain that this form of **treachery**[4] shall never endanger us again.

Hostilities exist. There is no blinking at the fact that our people, our territory, and our interests are in grave danger.

With confidence in our armed forces—with the unbounded determination of our people—we will gain the inevitable triumph—so help us God.

I ask that the Congress declare that since the unprovoked and **dastardly**[5] attack by Japan on Sunday, December 7, a state of war has existed between the United States and the Japanese Empire.

---

[2] **premeditated**—planned in advance.

[3] **righteous**—virtuous, upright.

[4] **treachery**—disloyalty, esp. to one's country; betrayal

[5] **dastardly**—cowardly; unscrupulous.

QUESTIONS TO CONSIDER

1. What led President Roosevelt to believe that the Japanese deliberately deceived the U.S.?

2. What assurance did President Roosevelt offer Congress that the U. S. would not be defeated?

Pearl Harbor and After

Pearl Harbor In a surprise attack, Japanese planes bombed Pearl Harbor.

◀ **Announcement** Newspapers were sold on the street corners announcing the bombing of Pearl Harbor.

U.S. Soldiers Even though the Japanese were demonized as the enemy, Japanese Americans enlisted and served in the U.S. military.

Patriotic feelings ran high after the bombing of Pearl Harbor.

"The Stranger Within Our Gates" and "The Fifth Column on the Coast"

Anti-Japanese hysteria swept the United States after Pearl Harbor, and much of it was directed toward Japanese Americans. Moreover, there was tremendous fear of a Japanese invasion of the West Coast, which had been declared a war zone under the control of the military. On January 19, 1942, Time magazine ran a leader called "The Stranger Within Our Gates," which raised fears of the Japanese Americans in Hawaii. On February 12, the enormously popular and influential columnist Walter Lippmann devoted his "Today and Tomorrow" column in the New York Herald Tribune to calling for the removal of Japanese Americans from the Pacific coast. Lippmann's article "The Fifth Column on the Coast" profoundly affected public opinion in favor of forcing Japanese Americans from the West Coast.

The Stranger Within Our Gates

Who was a friend, who was a foe? In Hawaii no one could be sure of the answer. Probably most of the Islands' 150,000 Japanese were loyal; perhaps, again, they were not. Last week Hawaii again suffered from the white man's old shortcoming—of not being able to tell one yellow man from another, nor the loyal from the disloyal. It was an overwhelming problem. For the Japs[1] were everywhere—behind shop counters in Honolulu, serving as gardeners on almost every island, cutting cane on all plantations, fishing off the coasts. Many of them were working on defense projects, many, as members of the Hawaiian Territorial Guard, were watching over power plants, parading in front of public buildings. The uniforms they wore were those of the U.S. Army, and only an arm badge, marked H.T.G.,[2] distinguished them from U.S. regulars.

In the minds of many of Hawaii's 105,000 *haoles* (whites), invasion loomed as a very real threat. What would the Islands' Japanese do then? Islanders who remembered that Jap high-school boys from Hawaii had helped pilot the planes that attacked Pearl Harbor looked uneasily at Hawaii's Japanese thousands going freely, **imperturbably**[3] about their business. What about the houseboy, the cop on the corner, the farmer down the road? What about the Japs set to guard the Islands?

In the New York *Times*, Newshawk Foster Hailey reported a discouraging conversation with one of the Army officers in Hawaii. Said the officer:

> "It is a terrific headache. You can't just pick up 150,000 persons and put them in a concentration camp. It would disrupt the life of the Islands and pose a bigger problem than any we are prepared to handle at the moment."

---

[1] Jap—derogatory term used to refer to the Japanese people.

[2] H.T.G.—Hawaiian Territorial Guard.

[3] **imperturbably**—tranquilly; calmly.

So as not to disrupt the life of the Islands, the military gave permission for two Jap papers to reappear, considered **resumption**[4] of Jap broadcasts from Hawaii's radio stations. Only thus could the Army convey its orders to non-English-speaking Japs.

QUESTIONS TO CONSIDER

1. Who is the stranger alluded to in the title?
2. What is the white man's shortcoming?
3. Why did the military permit Japanese newspapers to operate during the war?

The Fifth Column[5] *on the Coast*
by Walter Lippmann

The enemy **alien**[6] problem on the Pacific Coast, or, much more accurately, the fifth column problem, is very serious and it is very special. What makes it so serious and so special is that the Pacific Coast is in imminent danger of a combined attack from within and from without. The danger is not, as it would be in the inland centers, or perhaps even for the present on the Atlantic Coast, from sabotage alone. The peculiar danger of the Pacific Coast is in a Japanese raid accompanied by enemy action inside American territory. This combination can be very formidable indeed. For while the striking power of Japan from the sea and air might not in itself be overwhelming at any one point just now, Japan

---

[4] **resumption**—act of resuming or starting up again.

[5] Fifth Column—refers to traitors within a country who are helping the enemy through acts of sabotage.

[6] **alien**—a foreign-born citizen.

could strike a blow which might do irreparable damage if it were accompanied by the kind of organized sabotage to which this part of the country is specially vulnerable.

This is a sober statement of the situation, in fact, a report, based not on speculation but on what is known to have taken place and to be taking place in this area of the war. It is the fact that the Japanese navy has been **reconnoitering**[7] the Pacific Coast more or less continually and for a considerable period of time, testing and feeling out the American defenses. It is the fact that communication takes place between the enemy at sea and enemy agents on land. These are facts which we shall ignore or minimize at our peril. It also is the fact that since the outbreak of the Japanese war there has been no important sabotage on the Pacific Coast. From what we know about Hawaii and about the fifth column in Europe, this is not, as some have liked to think, a sign that there is nothing to be feared. It is a sign that the blow is well organized and that it is held back until it can be struck with maximum effect.

In preparing to repel the attack the Army and Navy have all the responsibility, but they are facing it with one hand tied down in Washington. I am sure I understand fully and appreciate thoroughly the unwillingness of Washington to adopt a policy of mass evacuation and mass **internment**[8] of all those who are technically enemy aliens. But I submit that Washington is not defining the problem on the Pacific Coast correctly and that therefore it is raising insoluble issues unnecessarily and failing to deal with the practical issues promptly. No one can ever hope to get the right answer unless he first asks the right questions.

---

[7] **reconnoitering**—surveying enemy territory for military purposes.

[8] **internment**—confinement during wartime.

The official approach to the danger is through a series of unrealities. There is the assumption that it is a problem of "enemy aliens." As a matter of fact, it is certainly also a problem of native-born American citizens. There is the assumption that a citizen may not be interfered with unless he has committed an overt act, or at least unless there is strong evidence that he is about to commit an overt act. There is the assumption that if the rights of a citizen are **abridged**[9] anywhere, they have been abridged everywhere. The effect of these assumptions has been to precipitate legalistic and ideological arguments between the military authorities out here and the civil authorities in Washington, and between the aroused citizenry of the coast and their fellow-countrymen in the interior.

A much simpler approach will, I believe, yield much more practical results. Forget for a moment all about enemy aliens, dual citizenship, naturalized citizens, native citizens of enemy alien parentage, and consider a warship in San Francisco Harbor, an airplant in Los Angeles, a general's headquarters at Oshkosh and an admiral's at Podunk. Then think of the lineal descendant, if there happened to be such a person, of George Washington, the Father of His Country, and consider what happens to Mr. Washington if he decides he would like to visit the warship, or take a walk in the airplane plant, or to drop in and photograph the general and the admiral in their quarters.

He is stopped by the sentry. He has to prove who he is. He has to prove that he has a good reason for doing what he wishes to do. He has to register, sign papers and wear an identification button. Then, perhaps, if he proves his case, he is escorted by an armed guard while

---

[9] **abridged**—diminished.

he does an errand, and until he has checked out of the place and his papers and his button have been returned. Have Mr. Washington's constitutional rights been abridged? Has he been denied the dignity of the human person? Has his loyalty been **impugned?**[10]

Now, it seems to me that this is, in principle and in general, the procedure which ought to be used for all persons in a zone which the military authorities regard as open to enemy attack. In that zone, as in the corridors of the general's headquarters or on the deck of the warship or within the gates of the airplane plant, every one should be compelled to prove that he has a good reason for being there, and no one should be allowed to come and go until he has proved that his business is necessary and consistent with the national defense.

In the vital and vulnerable areas it should be the rule that residence, employment, communication by telephone, telegraph, automobile and railroad are confined to licensed persons who are fully identified and whose activities are fully known to the authorities and to their neighbors. The Pacific Coast is officially a combat zone: some part of it may at any moment be a battlefield. Nobody's constitutional rights include the right to reside and do business on a battlefield. And nobody ought to be on a battlefield who has no good reason for being there. There is plenty of room elsewhere for him to exercise his rights.

This is in substance the system of policing which necessarily prevails in a war zone. By this system the constitutional and international questions about aliens

---

[10] **impugned**—attacked as false.

and citizens do not arise at the very place where they confuse the issues and prevent the taking of thorough measures of security. Under this system all persons are, in principle, treated alike. As a matter of national policy, there is no discrimination. But at the same time authorities on the spot in the threatened region are able to act decisively, and let the explanations, and the **reparations,**[11] come later.

This approach to the question bypasses the problem which, as I see it, has caused the trouble in Washington. For what Washington has been trying to find is a policy for dealing with all enemy aliens everywhere and all potential fifth columnists everywhere. Yet, a policy which may be wise in most parts of the country may be extremely foolhardy in a combat zone. Therefore, much the best thing to do is to recognize the Western combat zone as a territory quite different from the rest of the country, and then to set up in that zone a special regime. This has been done on the Bataan Peninsula, in Hawaii, in Alaska, in the Canal Zone. Why not also on the threatened west coast of the United States?

---

[11] **reparations**—amends made for a wrong or injury.

QUESTIONS TO CONSIDER

1. What is the problem outlined by Lippmann's article and what is his proposed solution?

2. Why do you think Lippmann's article about the "enemy alien problem" was so influential?

"Nisei¹ and Issei"² and "The Decision to Exclude"

In 1980, the U.S. government set up a commission to compile a comprehensive report on what happened to Japanese Americans during World War II. The Commission on Wartime Relocation and Internment of Civilians (CWRIC) interviewed more than 750 witnesses and reviewed thousands of government documents. Its report, Personal Justice Denied, *was issued in 1982 and is the most comprehensive study of why the U.S. government chose to intern Japanese Americans in 1942. The following excerpts are from the summary of the report. "Nisei and Issei"describes the situation of Japanese Americans in the wake of Pearl Harbor. "The Decision to Exclude" examines the factors and thinking that led to the exclusion and removal of ethnic Japanese from the West Coast.*

---

¹ Nisei—the first generation of ethnic Japanese born in the United States.

² Issei—the immigrant generation from Japan.

Nisei and Issei

On February 19, 1942, ten weeks after the Pearl Harbor attack, President Franklin D. Roosevelt signed Executive Order 9066, which gave to the Secretary of War and the military commanders to whom he delegated authority, the power to exclude any and all persons, citizens and aliens, from designated areas in order to provide security against sabotage, espionage and fifth column[3] activity. Shortly thereafter, all American citizens of Japanese descent were prohibited from living, working or traveling on the West Coast of the United States. The same prohibition applied to the generation of Japanese immigrants who, pursuant to federal law and despite long residence in the United States, were not permitted to become American citizens. Initially, this exclusion was to be carried out by "voluntary" relocation. That policy inevitably failed, and these American citizens and their alien parents were removed by the Army, first to "assembly centers"—temporary quarters at racetracks and fairgrounds—and then to "relocation centers"—bleak barrack camps mostly in desolate areas of the West. The camps were surrounded by barbed wire and guarded by military police. Departure was permitted only after a loyalty review on terms set, in consultation with the military, by the War Relocation Authority, the civilian agency that ran the camps. Many of those removed from the West Coast were eventually allowed to leave the camps to join the Army, go to college outside the West Coast or to whatever private employment was available. For a larger number, however, the war years were spent behind barbed wire; and for those who were released, the prohibition against returning to their homes and occupations on the West Coast was not lifted until December 1944.

---

[3] fifth column—refers to traitors within a country who aid the enemy through acts of sabotage.

This policy of exclusion, removal and detention was executed against 120,000 people without individual review, and exclusion was continued virtually without regard for their demonstrated loyalty to the United States. Congress was fully aware of and supported the policy of removal and detention; it sanctioned the exclusion by enacting a statute which made criminal the violation of orders issued pursuant to Executive Order 9066. The United States Supreme Court held the exclusion constitutionally permissible in the context of war, but struck down the **incarceration**[4] of admittedly loyal American citizens on the ground that it was not based on statutory authority.

All this was done despite the fact that not a single documented act of espionage, sabotage or fifth column activity was committed by an American citizen of Japanese ancestry or by a resident Japanese alien on the West Coast.

No mass exclusion or detention, in any part of the country, was ordered against American citizens of German or Italian descent. Official actions against enemy aliens of other nationalities were much more individualized and selective than those imposed on the ethnic Japanese.

The exclusion, removal and detention inflicted tremendous human cost. There was the obvious cost of homes and businesses sold or abandoned under circumstances of great distress, as well as injury to careers and professional advancement. But, most important, there was the loss of liberty and the personal **stigma**[5] of suspected disloyalty for thousands of people who knew themselves to be devoted to their country's cause and to its ideals but whose repeated protestations of loyalty were discounted—only to be demonstrated beyond any

---

[4] **incarceration**—confinement or imprisonment.

[5] **stigma**—a mark of shame or dishonor.

doubt by the record of Nisei soldiers, who returned from the battlefields of Europe as the most decorated and distinguished combat unit of World War II, and by the thousands of other Nisei who served against the enemy in the Pacific, mostly in military intelligence. The wounds of the exclusion and detention have healed in some respects, but the scars of that experience remain, painfully real in the minds of those who lived through the suffering and deprivation of the camps.

The personal injustice of excluding, removing and detaining loyal American citizens is **manifest.**[6] Such events are extraordinary and unique in American history. For every citizen and for American public life, they pose haunting questions about our country and its past. . . .

The Decision to Exclude

The context of the decision. First, the exclusion and removal were attacks on the ethnic Japanese which followed a long and ugly history of West Coast anti-Japanese **agitation**[7] and legislation. Antipathy and hostility toward the ethnic Japanese was a major factor of the public life of the West Coast states for more than forty years before Pearl Harbor. Under pressure from California, immigration from Japan had been severely restricted in 1908 and entirely prohibited in 1924. Japanese immigrants were barred from American citizenship, although their children born here were citizens by birth. California and the other western states prohibited Japanese immigrants from owning land. In part the hostility was economic, emerging in various white American groups who began to feel competition, particularly in agriculture, the principal occupation of the immigrants. The anti-Japanese agitation also fed on

---

[6] **manifest**—clear to see; obvious.
[7] **agitation**—the act of stirring up public feeling.

racial stereotypes and fears: the "yellow peril" of an unknown Asian culture achieving substantial influence on the Pacific Coast or of a Japanese population alleged to be growing far faster than the white population. This agitation and hostility persisted, even though the ethnic Japanese never exceeded three percent of the population of California, the state of greatest concentration.

The ethnic Japanese, small in number and with no political voice—the citizen generation was just reaching voting age in 1940—had become a convenient target for political **demagogues**,[8] and over the years all the major parties indulged in anti-Japanese rhetoric and programs. Political bullying was supported by organized interest groups who adopted anti-Japanese agitation as a consistent part of their program: the Native Sons and Daughters of the Golden West, the Joint Immigration Committee, the American Legion, the California State Federation of Labor and the California State Grange.

This agitation attacked a number of ethnic Japanese cultural traits or patterns which were woven into a bogus theory that the ethnic Japanese could not or would not assimilate or become "American." Dual citizenship, Shinto,[9] Japanese language schools, and the education of many ethnic Japanese children in Japan were all used as evidence. But as a matter of fact, Japan's laws on dual citizenship went no further than those of many European countries in claiming the allegiance of the children of its nationals born abroad. Only a small number of ethnic Japanese subscribed to Shinto, which in some forms included veneration of the Emperor. The language schools were not unlike those of other first-generation immigrants, and the return of some children to Japan for education was as much a reaction to hostile discrimination and an uncertain future as it

---

[8] **demagogues**—leaders who use popular prejudices and false promises in order to gain power.

[9] Shinto—religion originating in Japan.

was a commitment to the **mores**,[10] much less the political doctrines, of Japan. Nevertheless, in 1942 these popular misconceptions infected the views of a great many West Coast people who viewed the ethnic Japanese as alien and unassimilated.

Second, Japanese armies in the Pacific won a rapid, startling string of victories against the United States and its allies in the first months of World War II. On the same day as the attack on Pearl Harbor, the Japanese struck the Malay Peninsula, Hong Kong, Wake and Midway Islands and attacked the Philippines. The next day the Japanese Army invaded Thailand. On December 13 Guam fell; on December 24 and 25 the Japanese captured Wake Island and occupied Hong Kong. Manila was evacuated on December 27, and the American army retreated to the Bataan Peninsula. After three months the troops isolated in the Philippines were forced to surrender unconditionally—the worst American defeat since the Civil War. In January and February 1942, the military position of the United States in the Pacific was perilous. There was fear of Japanese attacks on the West Coast.

Next, contrary to the facts, there was a widespread belief, supported by a statement by Frank Knox, Secretary of the Navy, that the Pearl Harbor attack had been aided by sabotage and fifth column activity by ethnic Japanese in Hawaii. Shortly after Pearl Harbor the government knew that this was not true, but took no effective measures to disabuse public belief that disloyalty had contributed to massive American losses on December 7, 1941. Thus the country was unfairly led to believe that both American citizens of Japanese descent and resident Japanese aliens threatened American security.

Fourth, as anti-Japanese organizations began to speak out and rumors from Hawaii spread, West Coast

---

[10] **mores**—values.

politicians quickly took up the familiar anti-Japanese cry. The Congressional delegations in Washington organized themselves and pressed the War and Justice Departments and the President for stern measures to control the ethnic Japanese—moving quickly from control of aliens to evacuation and removal of citizens. In California, Governor Olson, Attorney General Warren, Mayor Bowron of Los Angeles and many local authorities joined the clamor. These opinions were not informed by any knowledge of actual military risks, rather they were stoked by virulent agitation which encountered little opposition. Only a few churchmen and academicians were prepared to defend the ethnic Japanese. There was little or no political risk in claiming that it was "better to be safe than sorry" and, as many did, that the best way for ethnic Japanese to prove their loyalty was to volunteer to enter detention. The press amplified the unreflective emotional excitement of the hour. Through late January and early February 1942, the rising clamor from the West Coast was heard within the federal government and its demands became more draconian.[11]

Making and justifying the decision. The exclusion of the ethnic Japanese from the West Coast was recommended to the Secretary of War, Henry L. Stimson, by Lieutenant General John L. DeWitt, Commanding General of the Western Defense Command with responsibility for West Coast security. President Roosevelt relied on Secretary Stimson's recommendations in issuing Executive Order 9066.

The justification given for the measure was military necessity. The claim of military necessity is most clearly set out in three places: General DeWitt's February 14, 1942, recommendation to Secretary Stimson for exclusion; General DeWitt's *Final Report: Japanese Evacuation*

---

[11] draconian—harsh, cruel.

from the West Coast, 1942; and the government's brief in the Supreme Court defending the Executive Order in *Hirabayashi v. United States*. General DeWitt's February 1942 recommendation presented the following rationale for the exclusion:

> In the war in which we are now engaged racial affinities are not severed by migration. The Japanese race is an enemy race and while many second and third generation Japanese born on United States soil, possessed of United States citizenship, have become "Americanized," the racial strains are undiluted. To conclude otherwise is to expect that children born of white parents on Japanese soil sever all racial affinity and become loyal Japanese subjects, ready to fight and, if necessary, to die for Japan in a war against the nation of their parents. That Japan is allied with Germany and Italy in this struggle is no ground for assuming that any Japanese, barred from assimilation by convention as he is, though born and raised in the United States, will not turn against this nation when the final test of loyalty comes. It, therefore, follows that along the vital Pacific Coast over 112,000 potential enemies, of Japanese extraction, are at large today. There are indications that these were organized and ready for concerted action at a favorable opportunity. The very fact that no sabotage has taken place to date is a disturbing and confirming indication that such action will be taken.

There are two unfounded justifications for exclusion expressed here: first, that ethnicity ultimately determines loyalty; second, that "indications" suggest that ethnic Japanese "are organized and ready for concerted action"—the best argument for this being the fact that it hadn't happened.

The first evaluation is not a military one but one for sociologists or historians. It runs counter to a basic premise on which the American nation of immigrants is built—that loyalty to the United States is a matter of dual choice and not determined by ties to an ancestral country. In the case of German Americans, the First World War demonstrated that race did not determine loyalty, and no negative assumption was made with regard to citizens of German or Italian descent during the Second World War. The second judgment was, by the General's own admission, unsupported by any evidence. General DeWitt's recommendation clearly does not provide a credible rationale, based on military expertise, for the necessity of exclusion.

In his 1943 *Final Report*, General DeWitt cited a number of factors in support of the exclusion decision: signaling from shore to enemy submarines; arms and contraband found by the FBI during raids on ethnic Japanese homes and businesses; dangers to the ethnic Japanese from **vigilantes;**[12] concentration of ethnic Japanese around or near militarily sensitive areas; the number of Japanese ethnic organizations on the coast which might shelter pro-Japanese attitudes or activities such as Emperor-worshipping Shinto; and the presence of the Kibei,[13] who had spent some time in Japan.

The first two items point to demonstrable military danger. But the reports of shore-to-ship signaling were investigated by the Federal Communications Commission, the agency with relevant expertise, and no identifiable cases of such signaling were substantiated. The FBI did confiscate arms and contraband from some ethnic Japanese, but most were items normally in the

---

[12] **vigilantes**—those who punish crime (without legal authority).

[13] Kibei—Issei who returned to Japan as children for education.

possession of any law-abiding civilian, and the FBI concluded that these searches had uncovered no dangerous persons that "we could not otherwise know about." Thus neither of these "facts" militarily justified exclusion.

There had been some acts of violence against ethnic Japanese on the West Coast and feeling against them ran high, but "protective custody" is not an acceptable rationale for exclusion. Protection against vigilantes is a civilian matter that would involve the military only in extreme cases. But there is no evidence that such extremity had been reached on the West Coast in early 1942. Moreover, "protective custody" could never justify exclusion and detention for months and years.

QUESTIONS TO CONSIDER

1. What were the steps leading from "voluntary" relocation to actual internment in relocation centers?

2. How many Nisei and Issei were detained and what evidence, if any, was there of espionage?

3. What justification was given for Japanese exclusion from the West Coast?

Apes and Others

BY JOHN DOWER

In the Time *magazine leader "The Stranger Within Our Gates" (see page 30) the author referred to Americans as suffering "from the white man's old shortcoming—of not being able to tell one yellow man from another." Overt racism was a key component of propaganda during the war in the Pacific. In 1986, the historian John Dower published a landmark study of this racism,* War Without Mercy: Race and Power in the Pacific War. *Dower scrutinized all types of media—newspapers, magazines, songs, cartoons, films, posters—to understand how Americans viewed their Japanese enemy. The following is an excerpt from* War Without Mercy *in which Dower examines how racial propaganda affected Japanese Americans.*

The treatment of Japanese Americans is a natural starting point for any study of the racial aspects of the war, for it reveals not merely the clear cut racial **stigmatization**[1] of the Japanese, but also the official endorsement this received. Under Executive Order 9066, signed by President Roosevelt on February 19, 1942,

---

[1] **stigmatization**—the branding of someone as disgraceful or shameful.

more than 110,000 persons of Japanese ancestry were removed from California, Oregon, and Washington and interned in ten camps in the interior of the United States. The president of the United States, the secretary of war, the U.S. military establishment, the Department of Justice and eventually the Supreme Court, and the U.S. Congress—all actively participated in enacting and upholding this policy. Similar internments were carried out in Canada, Mexico, and Peru. Such official consecration of anti-Japanese racism was profoundly symbolic: if every man, woman, and child of Japanese origin on the western coasts of the Americas was categorically identified by the highest quarters as a potential menace simply because of his or her ethnicity, then the real Japanese enemy abroad could only be perceived as a truly faceless, **monolithic**,[2] incorrigible, and stupendously **formidable**[3] foe.

Obviously, "blood told" where the Japanese—but not the Germans or Italians—were concerned, a point clearly articulated by some of the white Americans who supported the relocation of the Japanese. "Blood will tell," declared the mayor of Los Angeles in a public statement urging the government to move against Japanese Americans on the grounds that they were "unassimilable,"[4] and his West Coast counterparts agreed almost to a man; of all the mayors of large cities in the three westernmost states, only one (the mayor of Tacoma, Washington) opposed forced relocation. Secretary of War Henry Stimson, who assumed major responsibility for the decision to go ahead with Executive Order 9066, recorded in his diary for February 10, 1942, that in his estimation second-generation Japanese Americans were even more dangerous than their immigrant parents. They either

---

[2] **monolithic**—acting as a single, often rigid uniform whole.

[3] **formidable**—frightful; dreadful.

[4] "unassimilable"—not able to be absorbed into the cultural traditions of another group.

had to be removed from the coastal areas as part of a general evacuation, he continued, "or by frankly trying to put them out on the ground that their racial characteristics are such that we cannot understand or trust even the citizen Japanese. This latter is the fact but I am afraid it will make a tremendous hole in our constitutional system to apply it."

Such blood-will-tell racism was encoded in a variety of formulaic images and expressions. The *Los Angeles Times*, for instance, turned to reptilian metaphor: "A viper is nonetheless a viper wherever the egg is hatched—so a Japanese American, born of Japanese parents, grows up to be a Japanese not an American." In a telephone conversation shortly before the order for evacuation was signed by President Roosevelt, John J. McCloy, the influential assistant secretary of war, agreed with the more prosaic summation of the problem made by Lieutenant General John L. De Witt, commander of the Western Defense Command, to the effect that whereas Germans and Italians could be treated as individuals, "a Jap is a Jap." General De Witt, who administered the evacuation, still found this phrasing **felicitous**[5] over a year later when called upon to testify before a congressional committee as to why the incarcerated Japanese Americans, even bonafide citizens, still could not be allowed to return home. "A Jap's a Jap," he reiterated in public testimony in April 1943. "You can't change him by giving him a piece of paper." Indeed, in General De Witt's view, the menace posed by the Japanese could only be eliminated by destroying the Japanese as a race. In his testimony of early 1943, the general went on to state frankly that he was not worried about German or Italian nationals, "but the Japs we will be worried about all the time until they are wiped off the face of the map." This was, by then, familiar rhetoric in the nation's capital. A day before the president signed the executive order of February 19, a

---

[5] **felicitous**—well chosen; fitting; appropriate.

member of the House of Representatives had declared that the Japanese should be removed "even to the third and fourth generation." "Once a Jap, always a Jap," exclaimed John Rankin of Mississippi. "You can't any more regenerate a Jap than you can reverse the laws of nature."

Another manifestation of this most emotional level of anti-Japanese racism was the routine use of racial slang in the media and official memoranda as well as everyday discourse. "Nip" (from Nippon, the Japanese reading of the country's name) and especially "Jap" were routinely used in the daily press and major weeklies or monthlies such as *Time, Life, Newsweek*, and *Reader's Digest*. "Jap" was also extremely popular in the music world, where the scramble to turn out a memorable war song did not end with the release of tunes such as "The Remember Pearl Harbor March" and "Good-bye Mama, I'm Off to Yokohama." "Mow the Japs Down!" and "We've Got to Do a Job on the Japs, Baby" are fair samples of the wartime songs, although titles with internal rhymes on "Jap" were even more popular. These included "You're a Sap, Mister Jap," "Let's Take a Rap at the Jap," "They're Gonna Be Playing Taps on the Japs," and "We're Gonna Have to Slap the Dirty Little Jap." There was no real counterpart to this where Germany and Italy were concerned. "Nazis" was the common phrase for the German enemy. Cruder epithets for the Germans (heinies, Huns, Jerrys, Krauts) were used sparingly by comparison.

A characteristic feature of this level of anti-Japanese sentiment was the resort to nonhuman or subhuman representation, in which the Japanese were perceived as animals, reptiles, or insects (monkeys, baboons, gorillas, dogs, mice and rats, vipers and rattlesnakes, cockroaches, vermin—or, more indirectly, "the Japanese herd" and the like). The variety of such metaphors was so great that they sometimes seemed casual and almost original. On the contrary, they were well routinized as idioms of everyday discourse, and immensely consequential in their ultimate functions. At the simplest level, they dehumanized the Japanese and enlarged the chasm between "us" and "them" to the point where it was perceived to be virtually unbridgeable. As Pyle[6] matter-of-factly observed, the enemy in Europe "were still people." The Japanese were not, and in good part they were not because they were denied even the ordinary vocabularies of "being human."

For many Japanese Americans, the verbal stripping of their humanity was accompanied by humiliating treatment that reinforced the impression of being less than human. They were not merely driven from their homes and communities on the West Coast and rounded up like cattle, but actually forced to live in facilities meant for animals for weeks and even months before being moved to their final quarters in the relocation camps. In the state of Washington, two thousand Japanese Americans were crowded into a single filthy building in the Portland stockyard, where they slept on gunnysacks filled with straw. In California, evacuees were squeezed into stalls in the stables at racetracks such as Santa Anita and Tanforan. At the Santa Anita assembly center, which eventually housed eighty-five hundred Japanese Americans, only four days elapsed between the removal of the horses and the arrival of the first Japanese Americans; the only facilities for bathing were the horse showers, and here as elsewhere the stench of manure lingered indefinitely. Other evacuees were initially housed in horse or cattle stalls at various fairgrounds. At the Puyallup assembly center in Washington (which was called Camp Harmony), some were even lodged in converted pigpens. The only redeeming touch of grace in these circumstances lay in the dignity of the victims themselves.

[6] Ernie Pyle (1900–1945)—American journalist.

Looking upon the Japanese as animals, or a different species of some sort, was common at official levels in Washington and London before Pearl Harbor. A year and a half before the outbreak of the war, for instance, Churchill told Roosevelt that he was counting on the president "to keep that Japanese dog quiet in the Pacific." Secretary of War Henry Stimson picked up much the same image in October 1941 when arguing, as he had long done, in support of economic sanctions against Japan. When President Woodrow Wilson took a hard line against the Japanese in 1919, Stimson reminded the U.S. cabinet, they had retreated "like whipped puppies." During the war, "mad dogs" as well as "yellow dogs" were everyday epithets for the Japanese among the Western Allies. An American who spent considerable time in Japan between 1936 and late 1941 wrote a wartime article describing the evolution of one of his Japanese acquaintances from a moderate newsman into a "mad dog" ultranationalist military officer. "Mad dogs," he concluded, "are just insane animals that should be shot."

After his **repatriation**[7] from Japan in the first half of 1942, former U.S. Ambassador Joseph Grew, whom some Westerners regarded as an **oracle**[8] on things Japanese, drew equally upon the insect and animal kingdoms in his lectures about the enemy. He never attempted to conceal his personal respect and affection for certain "moderate" members of the cultured upper classes in Japan, but his most often-quoted statements about the Japanese people in general were those which also basically depersonalized them. For instance, Grew described Japan as a bustling hive of bees all servicing the queen (in real life, the emperor), and this image of the busy, buzzing swarm or its grounded counterpart

---

[7] **repatriation**—return to the country of origin.

[8] **oracle**—a person whose decisions are wise and authoritative.

the anthill was also popular with many other Western writers. An American sociologist explained on a wartime radio broadcast sponsored by General Electric that the Japanese were "a closely disciplined and conformist people—a veritable human bee-hive or ant-hill," in sharp contrast to the "independent and individualistic" Chinese. This, he continued, made Japan a "totalitarian" nation long before the word was invented to describe the fascist and Nazi systems. When Japanese ground forces lost the initiative in Southeast Asia and the Pacific, the antlike imagery was evoked in a somewhat different fashion. One reporter described the mid-war battles as a time when "the Japs turned into ants, the more you killed the more that kept coming." General Slim, Great Britain's commander in the epic Burma campaigns, used a similar metaphor in describing how his own forces finally seized the offensive. "We had kicked over the anthill," he wrote in his memoirs; "the ants were running about in confusion. Now was the time to stamp on them."

Former Ambassador Grew also spoke of the Japanese as sheep, easily led, which easily led one awkward publicist for the U.S. Navy to compare the frenzy of obedient Japanese soldiers to "angry sheep." *Yank*, the weekly magazine of the U.S. Army, referred to the "sheep-like subservience" of the Japanese (whom the magazine also called "stupid animal-slaves"), but by and large the sheep metaphor did not become a dominant one for the Japanese (in Churchill's menagerie, as in Stalin's, it was the Germans who were sheep). The more general description of the Japanese as a "herd," or possessing a "herd mentality," however, was routine. With various turns of phrase, the herd was one of the pet images of a group of distinguished Far Eastern experts assembled by Britain's Royal Institute of International Affairs to give advice on enemy Japan at the end of 1944. An Australian war correspondent went further, explaining that Japanese enlisted men not only behaved like, but also looked like, cattle. "Many of the Japanese soldiers I have seen have been primitive oxen-like clods with dulled eyes and foreheads an inch high," he wrote in a 1944 book directed to American readers. "They have stayed at their positions and died simply because they have been told to do so, and they haven't the intelligence to think for themselves."

Other, more random metaphors reinforced the impression of a sub-human enemy. Westerners writing about their personal experiences in Japan, for example, frequently described the Japanese as "hissing," a snake-like impression whether witting or not. As the Japanese extended their overseas imperium, even prior to Pearl Harbor, cartoonists depicted the country as an octopus grasping Asia in its tentacles. In *Know Your Enemy— Japan,* Frank Capra's team enlisted animators from the Walt Disney studio to present this as a central image, with the tentacles of octopus-Japan reaching out to plunge daggers into the hearts of neighboring lands, and groping toward the United States itself. The buck-toothed Japanese became a standard cartoon figure, prompting comparison to the Looney Tune creation Bugs Bunny; the Warner Brothers studio followed up on this with a short animated cartoon titled *Bugs Bunny Nips the Nips.*

Without question, however, the most common caricature of the Japanese by Westerners, writers and cartoonists alike, was the monkey or ape. Sir Alexander Cadogan, the influential permanent undersecretary of the British Foreign Office, routinely referred to the Japanese in his diary as "beastly little monkeys" and the like even before the war began (or alternatively, in February 1941, as "yellow dwarf slaves"). During the early months of the Japanese conquest of Southeast Asia, Western journalists referred to the "apes in khaki."

The **simian**[9] image had already become so integral to Western thinking by this time that when General Yamashita Tomoyuki's troops made their lightning move down the densely jungled Malay Peninsula to capture Singapore, rumors spread that they had accomplished this breathtaking advance by swinging from tree to tree. In mid-January of 1942, *Punch*, the celebrated British satirical magazine, drew upon the same utterly conventional image in a full-page cartoon entitled "The Monkey Folk" that depicted monkeys swinging through the jungle with helmets on their heads and rifles slung over their shoulders. In much the same way, U.S. Marines in the combat zones made jokes about tossing a grenade into a tree and blasting out "three monkeys—two bucktooths and a real specimen," a witticism that the *New Yorker* carried to its upper-class readership in cartoon form late in 1942 and *Reader's Digest* reproduced for its own huge audience soon after. It portrayed white riflemen lying in firing position in a dense jungle, where the trees were full of monkeys along with several Japanese snipers. "Careful now," one white soldier is saying to another, "—only those in uniform." An American radio broadcaster informed his audience early in the war that it was appropriate to regard the Japanese as monkeys for two reasons: first, the monkey in the zoo imitates his trainer; secondly, "under his fur, he's still a savage little beast."

Among the Allied war leaders, Admiral Halsey was the most notorious for making outrageous and virulently racist remarks about the Japanese enemy in public. Many of his slogans and pronouncements bordered on advocacy of genocide. Although he came under criticism for his **intemperate**[10] remarks, and was even accused of being drunk in public, Halsey was immensely popular among his men and naturally

---

[9] **simian**—relating to or resembling monkeys or apes.

[10] **intemperate**—excessive; unreasonable.

attracted good press coverage. His favorite phrase for the Japanese was "yellow bastards," and in general he found the color allusion irresistible. Simian metaphors, however, ran a close second in his **diatribes**.[11] Even in his postwar memoirs, Halsey described the Japanese as "stupid animals" and referred to them as "monkey-men." During the war he spoke of the "yellow monkeys," and in one outburst declared that he was "rarin' to go" on a new naval operation "to get some more Monkey meat." He also told a news conference early in 1945 that he believed the "Chinese proverb" about the origin of the Japanese race, according to which "the Japanese were a product of mating between female apes and the worst Chinese criminals who had been banished from China by a benevolent emperor." These comments were naturally picked up in Japan, as Halsey fully intended them to be, and on occasion prompted lame responses in kind. A Japanese propaganda broadcast, for example, referred to the white Allies as "albino apes." Halsey's well-publicized comment, after the Japanese Navy had been placed on the defensive, that "the Japs are losing their grip, even with their tails," led a zookeeper in Tokyo to announce he was keeping a cage in the monkey house reserved for the admiral.

---

[11] **diatribes**—bitter and abusive criticisms.

QUESTIONS TO CONSIDER

1. In what ways did Americans strip the Japanese Americans of their humanity during World War II?

2. What is "blood-will-tell" racism? Can you think of other groups besides the Japanese who have been subjected to this sort of racism?

3. Do you think it's acceptable to depict the enemy as an animal if such a representation will improve national defense? Why or why not?

A Birthright Renounced[1]

BY JOSEPH KURIHARA

Joseph Kurihara was born in Hawaii of Japanese parents. Kurihara served in the United States Army during World War I and, thinking only to serve his country when war broke out again in 1941, he tried to get various defense-related jobs. In the end he was denied employment and eventually interned at the camp at Manzanar. Kurihara was horrified at the way his country had treated him, and after the war renounced his American citizenship and emigrated to Japan, a country he had never visited. The following is an excerpt from Kurihara's account of his experiences during World War II.

I was born in the little village of Hanamaulu, Kauai, on the first day of January 1895. At the age of two, my parents moved to Honolulu. . . . We, the boys of **conglomerated**[2] races, were brought up under the careful guidance of American teachers, strictly following the

---

[1] **renounced**—gave up, abandoned, resigned from.

[2] **conglomerated**—gathered into a mass.

principle of American democracy. Let it be white, black, brown, or yellow, we were all treated alike. This glorious paradise of the Pacific was the true melting pot of human races. . . .

[In order to study medicine, Kurihara moved to California. There he encountered many instances of discrimination, as for example, in Sacramento.] As my friend and I were ambulating in the residential district, a short distance away from the Japanese center, something came whizzing by, and then another and another. We noticed they were rocks being thrown at us by a number of youngsters. As we went toward them, they ran and hid. It was really aggravating. Feeling perplexed, I asked my friend, "Why do they attack us in such a manner?" He answered, "It's discrimination." No such thing ever happened where I came from. It was disgusting. At the time, I felt homesick for my good old native land, Hawaii. . . .

Disregarding the conditions, I pursued my studies for two years. . . . Unexpectedly, my friend from Sacramento called and persuaded me to go east, Michigan as the destination. He vouched to me that the American people east of Chicago were very friendly and kind. They did not discriminate just because we were Japanese. They would treat us as one of their equals. I could not believe it, but the news was very tempting after experiencing much unpleasantness for two years. . . .

[Soon after arriving in Michigan, Kurihara decided to join the army and reported to Camp Custer.] During this training period, I was befriended by many, amongst whom were Dr. Homer Knight of Charlotte and Mr. William Green, president of the Green Advertising Company of Detroit. I made several visits to their homes. On every occasion, I was treated like a prince. I felt very happy. Knowing that they were going out of the way to make me happy, I solemnly vouched to fight and die for the U.S. and those good people, whose genuine kindness touched the very bottom of my heart. . . . In California my **animosities**[3] against the Californians were growing with ever increasing intensity, but here in Michigan, my liking for the American people was getting the best of me. . . .

[Kurihara enlisted[4] and was sent to France, where his unit was ordered to march sixty-two kilometers to the front.] After our arrival, we made preparations for the drive on Metz, digging gun pits and hauling ammunition. We waded through mud and slept in a dugout, bothered by rats and dripping water that soaked through the earth on our bunks. Water was scarce, making a bath a luxury. The sticky mud became part of our breeches. I felt so dirty I would have given my last penny for a bath. . . .

At the front, while making extensive preparation for the drive on Metz, someone gave away the secret and told us that an armistice was going to be declared on November 11. Oh, what a happy tiding it was to us all! Thank God, peace again would be restored to mankind. . . .

For seven months I was stationed in Coblenz with the army of occupation. . . . I found out that the German people were just as much human as any other race. They were no more beasts than the rest of the people in this world. I learned to like these people because they were kind and sincere. A little German girl voluntarily washed my laundry and returned it neatly ironed. So I, in return, gave little Freida chocolate candies and other sweets, including some canned foods I secured from the supply sergeant. Soap was very scarce in Germany, so this too I requisitioned and gave to her.

At every mealtime, the little German girls and boys were lining the walk to the garbage can for whatever

---

[3] **animosities**—resentments; hostilities.

[4] Kurihara enlisted and served in World War I.

scraps the boys were throwing away. I could not bear to see these little ones suffer, so I always made it my duty to ask for as much as my plate would hold and gave it to them. . . .

I took advantage of the two-week furlough being granted during my stay in Germany and visited Cologne, Brussels, Ypres, Paris and numerous other historically important places. Wherever I went, I saw the ugly scars of war, reminding me of the cannibalistic deeds of man only more cruel and complete in civilized manner. It was horrible to think that the more the world progresses in science, the more devilish it gets. I shuddered from thoughts what the next war would be. . . .

[During the next two decades, Kurihara pursued various activities in the Los Angeles area. He completed degree programs at California Community College and Southwestern University, worked as an accountant in the Japanese community, operated small produce businesses, studied television and navigation, and worked as a navigator on a tuna clipper.]

On the day when war broke out (December 7), we were fishing around the Galapagos Islands. Naval orders from Panama instructed all American vessels on the coast to put in at once into Panama or into any friendly port. . . . On the way above Cedros Islands, which are approximately three hundred miles south of San Diego, we saw American planes scouting the sea and reporting the movements of all vessels. It was thrilling to see them flying around to determine the name of the boat. I felt proud of them. Above all I was happy to be back in sight of America without a mishap.

We entered San Diego Bay immediately after daybreak. In the bay, the boat was stopped and several officers in naval uniforms came aboard. They scrutinized the papers, and finding them satisfactory, they left, taking three of us along—two Portuguese and myself.

We were taken to the naval wharf and awaited orders, but none came. Around nine-thirty, we again were asked to board the official launch, and this time were taken back to our own ship. No sooner had I boarded the ship, a plain-clothes man yelled, "Hey! you Jap, I want some information. You better tell me everything, or I'll kick you in the___." My blood boiled. I felt like clubbing his head off. It was just a hat-rack and nothing more.

"What did you call me? If you want any information from me, you better learn to address a man properly."

"Is that so?"

"Yes, and most positively."

[After being kept waiting for three hours without lunch, Kurihara was again questioned]:

"What do you think of the war?"

"Terrible."

"Who do you think will win this war?"

"Who knows. God only knows."

"Do you think Japan has the materials she needs to wage this war?"

"I never was there, so your guess is just as good as mine."

"Are you a navigator?"

"Yes, I navigated boats for the last eight years."

"Have you a navigator's license?"

"No, but I have a captain's license, which gives me the right to navigate."

"Have you been a good American citizen?"

"I was and I am."

"Will you fight for this country?"

"If I am needed, I am ready."

"Were you a soldier of any country?"

"Yes, I am a veteran of the Foreign War, U.S. Army."

"Okay, that's all. If you hear or notice anything suspicious, please report the matter to me."

"I will."

"You may go."

I was really famished. I had no other thought but to satisfy my hunger. . . .

I went to the employment department of the Consolidated Aircraft Corporation to apply for a position as navigator. I wanted to do my share as an American citizen. The best and most useful place which I could apply my knowledge was as a navigator to navigate the bombers across the country to New York, from thence to England. I had absolute confidence in this work. . . .

[At Consolidated Aircraft, Kurihara was told to call back every day although other applicants were being notified by mail. When he tried to get a job with the merchant marines, he was informed that they were not employing any Japanese. Next, he tried California Shipbuilding, where the employment manager said Kurihara would not be happy because of discrimination from the other employees. Finally, he went to Bethlehem Steel and was not even admitted into the yard by the guard at the gate.]

A friend from Terminal Island requested a loan of $500. Being a very trustworthy person, I went to the bank to withdraw the requested amount to help. The bank manager told me I had to get an okay from the F.B.I. office before he could let me have the money. If I were an alien, probably I could see the reason why, but since I am a citizen, I could not. My account was not frozen. We argued for awhile. He knew I was right, but he was afraid to give it to me. I decided to see the F.B.I.

[At the FBI office, an officer asked him many of the same questions he had answered after being taken from his boat. Impatient, Kurihara asked him what the questions had to do with the withdrawal.]

One of the other officers, a husky and powerful looking gentleman (a **ruffian**[5] is better suited to him here), interrupted and said, "Say, you, I do not like your attitude. Understand?"

"Maybe you don't like my attitude, and if you want to know, I don't like the foolish questions I am asked."

"You don't? Well, you better like it."

It looked for a moment as if he was going to strike. I paid no attention to his threatening manner. I kept sitting calmly. Then the first officer asked me if I had any proof to show that I was an American citizen. In answer to this question, I pulled out a folder in my pocket and unfolded it. This folder was purposely made to hold the Honorable Discharge Certificate of the U.S. Army. This the officers unfailingly noticed. I handed my birth certificate to the officer which he **scrutinized**.[6] The other officer at once changed his bullish attitude and spoke more politely thereafter. Before departing, the officer told me he didn't like it because my voice was rather loud. I told him it was my natural voice. He understood, and we parted with no harm done. [Eventually, Kurihara was permitted to withdraw the money.]

Having nothing to do with plenty of time, I wrote to my cousin discussing the war, and in it I denounced the Japanese militarists in no uncertain words. I do not believe in war. It is the most horrible thing on earth. I've seen the sufferings of the poor German girls and boys while in Coblenz, the destroyed cities and towns throughout the front, and the unendurable hardships the poor soldier boys had to go through. . . .

Since the last ray of hope had vanished, I decided to return to Los Angeles. During the ensuing week, Terminal Island was thrown into turmoil. All able-bodied men went to help the poor women on whose

---

[5] **ruffian**—a coarse, brutal person.

[6] **scrutinized**—examined very closely or critically.

heads the world came crashing down. [All Japanese, both aliens and citizens, had been ordered to evacuate from the West Coast. In the case of Terminal Island, the men were taken away first.]

It was really cruel and harsh. To pack and evacuate in forty-eight hours was an impossibility. Seeing mothers completely bewildered with children crying from want and care, the peddlers taking advantage and offering prices next to robbery, made me feel like murdering those responsible without the slightest **compunction**[7] in my heart.

The parents might have been aliens, but the children were all American citizens. Did the government of the United States intend to ignore their rights, regardless of their citizenship? Those beautiful furnitures, which the parents bought to please their sons and daughters, costing hundreds of dollars, were robbed of them at the single command—"Evacuate!" Here my first doubt of American Democracy had crept into the far corners of my heart with the sting that I could not forget.

Democracy had been my political affiliation before, and the first vote I casted. Having had absolute confidence in democracy, I could not believe my very eyes of what I had seen that day. America, the standard bearer of democracy had committed the most **heinous**[8] crime in its history, indelibly imprinting in my mind, as well as in the minds of those children, the dread that even democracy is a demon in time of war. It is my sincere desire to see this government of the United States some day repair the wrong in full.

When the Army took command of the Western Defense area, it relieved me greatly because I really believed it was capable of handling the situation. There would be no more hysteria, and we Japanese, especially

---

[7] **compunction**—distress or anxiety arising from guilt.

[8] **heinous**—shockingly evil.

the Niseis [Japanese born in the United States] could settle down and go to work. But no sooner after it did, our rights as American citizens were shattered by General DeWitt. Frankly, I doubt his ability as a general.

[Kurihara had expected the Japanese American Citizens League to contest the evacuation orders. Instead, he was angered by what he considered a lack of courage on the part of the J.A.C.L. leaders. At this time, he vowed to challenge them in the camps.]

On March 23, 1942, I left for Manzanar [an internment camp in southeastern California] with the second contingent of volunteers. I wanted to be there first since I was single and free to help those arriving later with children, so they could be comfortably installed.

The camp was in topsy-turvy condition. Life was really discouraging during the first two months. The wind blew with such ferocity that at times I thought the building was going to be carried away. Dust were everywhere. Sandstorms were so bad it obscured the sun. We, in fact, slept in the dust, breathed the dust, and ate the dust. Bath houses were in the stage of blue-print. For two weeks we had to go without a bath.

Manzanar enjoyed peace and tranquility for several months. It would have continued to enjoy peace and tranquility had not the J.A.C.L. **brazenly**[9] made its appearance after it was quietly organized by those spineless leaders. . . . They called a meeting which I attended to fulfill the vow I had made to crush them wherever I met them. . . . Instantly, when the floor was opened for general discussion, I took the floor and started bombarding and blasting the organization to bits. The entire floor was electrified. After some verbal blasting I gave to Talkative Slocum (Tokutaro Nishimura), who not only interrupted my speech but threw mud at me, the hall resounded with such cheers, whistling and

---

[9] **brazenly**—shamelessly.

stamping, it was said the noise was heard throughout the center. I had turned the table with unquestionable success. . . .

[A few days after a national convention of the J.A.C.L. was held at Salt Lake City, one of its leaders was severely beaten. Harry Ueno was arrested on suspicion. Kurihara took up the fight to have him released. This resulted in what was called the "Manzanar Incident." Demonstrators denouncing J.A.C.L. leaders and the camp administration began rioting. Soldiers then fired machine guns into the crowd, wounding ten internees and killing two. Kurihara was arrested and thrown into jail. He was then taken to another internment camp in Moab, Utah.]

Mr. R. R. Best, the director, treated us very kindly. For a long time, we ate the same food in the same mess hall with the soldiers, enjoying the best. I have absolutely no complaint to make under this humane treatment we received. If all directors were like Mr. Best, I am sure the Japanese would have no cause to revolt. Such is the true and sincere opinion I entertained both in Moab and at Leupp, Arizona, under his administration. . . .

Mr. Robertson, who succeeded Mr. Best, was very kind to us. He was really a God-send. Though he was slightly more exacting, like Mr. Best he went out of his way to see that the boys got everything they had coming. I again commenced to see the beautiful side of the American people, which was completely submerged with hatred. The bitterness which dominated my feelings for months after the killing of those two innocent boys at Manzanar was so great I could have murdered any white man as if he were an animal. Was it time that healed it? No, it was the kindness of these two real Americans.

Through Mr. Robertson's efforts, we were transferred to Tule Lake on December 6, 1943. We were thrown into the stockade upon arrival, out of which I was released three days later and enjoyed the freedom of the camp once more. The faces of the little children were really consoling. If we only could be like them, this world would be void of trouble, I thought. . . .

In the face of my cooling animosity against this country, my American friends, especially Mr. Best, no doubt must have wondered why I had renounced my citizenship. This decision was not that of today or that of yesterday. It dates back to the day when General DeWitt ordered evacuation. It was confirmed when he flatly refused to listen even to the voices of the former World War veterans, and it was doubly confirmed as I entered Manzanar. We who already had proven our loyalty by serving in the last World War should have been spared. The veterans asked for special consideration, but their requests were denied. They too had to evacuate like the rest of the Japanese people, as if they were aliens.

I did not expect this of the Army. When the Western Defense Command assumed the responsibilities of the West Coast, I expected that, at least, the Niseis would be allowed to remain. But to General DeWitt, we were all alike. "A Jap is a Jap. Once a Jap, always a Jap." He must have felt great when he phrased it, but today no doubt he must be feeling ashamed of it. A great man does not manifest his feelings in such **contemptuous**[10] words. I then swore to become a Jap one hundred percent, and never to do another day's work to help this country fight this war. My decision to renounce my citizenship there and then was definite and absolute. . . .

[In February of 1946, Kurihara sailed to Japan, a country he had not yet even visited.]

---

[10] **contemptuous**—showing disdain or disrespect.

QUESTIONS TO CONSIDER

1. For Kurihara, what was the main difference between the West Coast and the Midwest?

2. What events and circumstances led Kurihara to question American democracy? Why did he believe that democracy became a "demon" in wartime?

3. Why did Kurihara rebel against the J.A.C.L. (Japanese-American Citizens League)?

4. Considering that Kurihara spoke highly of Mr. Best and Mr. Robertson, two of the camp directors, why did he ultimately renounce his citizenship and move to Japan?

Evacuation and Internment

Executive Order 9066

Walter Lippmann's article (see page 31) brought public pressure to a head, and congressional leaders pressed the president to act against the perceived threat posed by Japanese Americans. On February 19, 1942, President Roosevelt signed Executive Order 9066, which authorized the military to exclude people from "prescribed military areas" and created the War Relocation Authority (WRA). The WRA ordered Japanese Americans to evacuate the coastal areas; however, other states refused to allow Japanese Americans to move there. The WRA then decided that the evacuees would be forcibly resettled into concentration camps. On April 30, the Civilian Exclusion Orders (see page 81) were posted ordering Japanese Americans to leave their homes and assemble for internment.

WHEREAS the successful prosecution of the war requires every possible protection against espionage and against sabotage to national defense material, national defense premises, and national defense utilities as defined in Section 4, Act of April 20, 1918, 40 Stat. 533, as amended by the Act of November 30, 1940, 54 Stat. 1220, and the Act of August 21, 1941, 55 Stat. 655 (U. S. C., Title 50, Sec. 104):

NOW, THEREFORE, by virtue of the authority vested in me as President of the United States, and Commander in Chief of the Army and Navy, I hereby authorize and direct the Secretary of War, and the Military Commanders who he may from time to time designate, whenever he or any designated Commander deems such action necessary or desirable, to prescribe military areas in such places and of such extent as he or the appropriate Military Commander may determine, from which any or all persons may be excluded, and with respect to which, the right of any person to enter, remain in, or leave shall be subject to whatever restrictions the Secretary of War or the appropriate Military Commander may impose in his **discretion**.[1] The Secretary of War is hereby authorized to provide for residents of any such area who are excluded therefrom, such transportation, food, shelter, and other accommodations as may be necessary, in the judgment of the Secretary of War or the said Military Commander, and until other arrangements are made, to accomplish the purpose of this order. The designation of military areas in any region or locality shall **supersede**[2] designations of prohibited and restricted areas by the Attorney General under the Proclamations of December 7 and 8, 1941, and shall supersede the responsibility and authority of the Attorney General under the said Proclamations in respect of such prohibited and restricted areas.

I hereby further authorize and direct the Secretary of War and the said Military Commanders to take such other steps as he or the appropriate Military Commander may deem advisable to enforce compliance

---

[1] **discretion**—individual choice or judgment.

[2] **supersede**—to be superior to; to force out of use.

with the restrictions applicable to each Military area hereinabove authorized to be designated, including the use of Federal troops and other Federal Agencies, with authority to accept assistance of state and local agencies.

I hereby further authorize and direct all Executive Departments, independent establishments and other Federal Agencies, to assist the Secretary of War or the said Military Commanders in carrying out this Executive Order, including the furnishing of medical aid, hospitalization, food, clothing, transportation, use of land, shelter, and other supplies, equipment, utilities, facilities, and services.

This order shall not be construed as modifying or limiting in any way the authority heretofore granted under Executive Order No. 8972, dated December 12, 1941, nor shall it be construed as limiting or modifying the duty and responsibility of the Federal Bureau of Investigation, with respect to the investigation of alleged acts of sabotage or the duty and responsibility of the Attorney General and the Department of Justice under the Proclamations of December 7 and 8, 1941, prescribing regulations for the conduct and control of alien enemies, except as such duty and responsibility is superseded by the designation of military areas hereunder.

THE WHITE HOUSE
February 19, 1942

QUESTIONS TO CONSIDER

1. What, in your view, is the most meaningful sentence or passage from this Executive Order? Explain why you think so.

2. What, if anything, suggests that this order was directed at Japanese Americans and that it was suspending their civil rights?

"The Decision to Detain" and "The Effect of the Exclusion and Detention"[1]

Following the Civilian Exclusion Order, Japanese-American families had to register at control centers where each was given a number. After packing up and selling off their possessions, the families were bused from the control center to an assembly center, where they were housed until the camps were ready to receive their prisoners. Special military trains took 112,000 people, two-thirds of them American citizens, to a home behind barbed wire. The following excerpts are from Personal Justice Denied, *the 1982 report of the Commission on Wartime Relocation and Internment of Civilians. "The Decision to Detain" describes the process by which Executive Order 9066 (see page 70) led to the mass evacuation and internment of Japanese Americans. "The Effect of the Exclusion and Detention" examines the experience of detention and its effect on Japanese Americans.*

---

[1] **detention**—the act of holding back or keeping in custody.

The Decision to Detain

With the signing of Executive Order 9066, the course of the President and the War Department was set: American citizens and alien residents of Japanese ancestry would be compelled to leave the West Coast on the basis of wartime military necessity. For the War Department and the Western Defense Command, the problem became primarily one of method and operation, not basic policy. General DeWitt first tried "voluntary" resettlement: the ethnic Japanese were to move outside the restricted military zones of the West Coast but otherwise were free to go wherever they chose. From a military standpoint this policy was bizarre, and it was utterly impractical. If the ethnic Japanese had been excluded because they were potential **saboteurs**[2] and spies, any such danger was not extinguished by leaving them at large in the interior where there were, of course, innumerable dams, power lines, bridges and war industries to be disrupted or spied upon. Conceivably sabotage in the interior could be synchronized with a Japanese raid or invasion for a powerful fifth column effect. This raises serious doubts as to how grave the War Department believed the supposed threat to be. Indeed, the implications were not lost on the citizens and politicians of the interior western states, who objected in the belief that people who threatened wartime security in California were equally dangerous in Wyoming and Idaho.

The War Relocation Authority (WRA), the civilian agency created by the President to supervise the relocation and initially directed by Milton Eisenhower, proceeded on the premise that the vast majority of evacuees were law-abiding and loyal, and that, once off the West Coast, they should be returned quickly to conditions

---

[2] **saboteurs**—civilians or enemy agents who carry out actions designed to hinder a nation's war effort.

approximating normal life. This view was strenuously opposed by the people and politicians of the mountain states. In April 1942, Milton Eisenhower met with the governors and officials of the mountain states. They objected to California using the interior states as a "dumping ground" for a California "problem." They argued that people in their states were so bitter over the voluntary evacuation that unguarded evacuees would face physical danger. They wanted guarantees that the government would forbid evacuees to acquire land and that it would remove them at the end of the war. Again and again, detention camps for evacuees were urged. The consensus was that a plan for reception centers was acceptable so long as the evacuees remained under guard within the centers.

In the circumstances, Milton Eisenhower decided that the plan to move the evacuees into private employment would be abandoned, at least temporarily. The War Relocation Authority dropped resettlement and adopted confinement. Notwithstanding WRA's belief that evacuees should be returned to normal productive life, it had, in effect, become their jailer. The politicians of the interior states had achieved the program of detention.

The evacuees were to be held in camps behind barbed wire and released only with government approval. For this course of action no military justification was proffered. Instead, the WRA contended that these steps were necessary for the benefit of evacuees and that controls on their departure were designed to assure they would not be mistreated by other Americans on leaving the camps.

It follows from the conclusion that there was no justification in military necessity for the exclusion, that there was no basis for the detention.

The Effect of the Exclusion and Detention

The history of the relocation camps and the assembly centers that preceded them is one of suffering and deprivation visited on people against whom no charges were, or could have been, brought. The Commission hearing record is full of poignant, searing testimony that recounts the economic and personal losses and injury caused by the exclusion and the deprivations of detention. No summary can do this testimony justice.

Families could take to the assembly centers and the camps only what they could carry. Camp living conditions were **Spartan**.[3] People were housed in tar-papered barrack rooms of no more than 20 by 24 feet. Each room housed a family, regardless of family size. Construction was often shoddy. Privacy was practically impossible and furnishings were minimal. Eating and bathing were in mass facilities. Under continuing pressure from those who blindly held to the belief that evacuees harbored disloyal intentions, the wages paid for work at the camps were kept to the minimal level of $12 a month for unskilled labor, rising to $19 a month for professional employees. Mass living prevented normal family communication and activities. Heads of families, no longer providing food and shelter, found their authority to lead and to discipline diminished.

The normal functions of community life continued but almost always under a handicap—doctors were in short supply; schools which taught typing had no typewriters and worked from hand-me-down school books; there were not enough jobs.

The camp experience carried a **stigma**[4] that no other Americans suffered. The evacuees themselves expressed the indignity of their conditions with particular power:

---

[3] **Spartan**—marked by a lack of comfort and luxury.

[4] **stigma**—a mark of shame or dishonor.

On May 16, 1942, my mother, two sisters, niece, nephew, and I left . . . by train. Father joined us later. Brother left earlier by bus. We took whatever we could carry. So much we left behind, but the most valuable thing I lost was my freedom.

Henry went to the Control Station to register the family. He came home with twenty tags, all numbered 10710, tags to be attached to each piece of baggage, and one to hang from our coat lapels. From then on, we were known as Family #10710.

The government's efforts to "Americanize" the children in the camps were bitterly ironic:

An oft-repeated ritual in relocation camp schools . . . was the salute to the flag followed by the singing of "My country, 'tis of thee, sweet land of liberty"—a ceremony Caucasian teachers found embarrassingly awkward if not cruelly poignant in the austere prison-camp setting.

In some ways, I suppose, my life was not too different from a lot of kids in America between the years 1942 and 1945. I spent a good part of my time playing with my brothers and friends, learned to shoot marbles, watched sandlot baseball and envied the older kids who wore Boy Scout uniforms. We shared with the rest of America the same movies, screen heroes and listened to the same heart-rending songs of the forties. We imported much of America into the camps because, after all, we were Americans. Through imitation of my brothers, who attended grade school within the camp, I learned the salute to the flag by the time I was five years old. I was learning, as best one could learn in

Manzanar, what it meant to live in America. But, I was also learning the sometimes bitter price one has to pay for it.

After the war, through the Japanese American Evacuation Claims Act, the government attempted to compensate for the losses of real and personal property; inevitably that effort did not secure full or fair compensation. There were many kinds of injury the Evacuation Claims Act made no attempt to compensate: the stigma placed on people who fell under the exclusion and relocation orders; the deprivation of liberty suffered during detention; the psychological impact of exclusion and relocation; the breakdown of family structure; the loss of earnings or profits; physical injury or illness during detention.

QUESTIONS TO CONSIDER

1. Why was the idea of voluntary evacuation and resettlement of Japanese Americans abandoned?

2. What was family #10710 and what were the conditions they were likely to have faced in the relocation camp?

3. What attempts were made to "Americanize" the children? Why were these steps taken?

Rush to Evacuate

Sale Japanese Americans were ordered to evacuate immediately. This measure forced them to sell their property and belongings at distress prices, costing families untold amounts.

Notices Evacuation notices were posted in public places, ordering Japanese to report to relocation centers.

Headquarters
Western Defense Command
and Fourth Army

Presidio of San Francisco, California
May 10, 1942

Civilian Exclusion Order No. 57

1. Pursuant to the provisions of Public Proclamations Nos. 1 and 2, this Headquarters, dated March 2, 1942, and March 16, 1942, respectively, it is hereby ordered that from and after 12 o'clock noon, P.W.T., of Saturday, May 16, 1942, all persons of Japanese ancestry, both alien and non-alien, be excluded from that portion of Military Area No. 1 described as follows:

> All that portion of the County of King, State of Washington, within the boundary beginning at the intersection of Roosevelt Way and East Eighty-fifth Street; thence easterly along East Eighty-fifth Street and East Eighty-fifth Street extended to Lake Washington; thence southerly along the shoreline of Lake Washington to the point at which Yesler Way meets Lake Washington; thence westerly along Yesler Way to Fifteenth Avenue; thence northerly on Fifteenth Avenue to East Madison Street; thence southwesterly on East Madison Street to Fifth Avenue; thence northwesterly along Fifth Avenue to Westlake Avenue; thence northerly along Westlake Avenue to Virginia Street; thence northeasterly along Virginia Street to Fairview Avenue North; thence northerly along Fairview Avenue North to Eastlake Avenue; thence northerly along Eastlake Avenue to Roosevelt Way; thence northerly along Roosevelt Way to the point of beginning.

2. A responsible member of each family, and each individual living alone, in the above described area will report between the hours of 8:00 A. M. and 5:00 P. M., Monday, May 11, 1942, or during the same hours on Tuesday, May 12, 1942, to the Civil Control Station located at:

> Christian Youth Center,
> 2203 East Madison Street,
> Seattle, Washington.

3. Any person subject to this order who fails to comply with any of its provisions or with the provisions of published instructions pertaining hereto or who is found in the above area after 12 o'clock noon, P.W.T., of Saturday, May 16, 1942, will be liable to the criminal penalties provided by Public Law No. 503, 77th Congress, approved March 21, 1942, entitled "An Act to Provide a Penalty for Violation of Restrictions or Orders with Respect to Persons Entering, Remaining in, Leaving or Committing any Act in Military Areas or Zones," and alien Japanese will be subject to immediate apprehension and internment.

4. All persons within the bounds of an established Assembly Center pursuant to instructions from this Headquarters are excepted from the provisions of this order while those persons are in such Assembly Center.

> J. L. DeWitt
> Lieutenant General, U. S. Army
> Commanding

▲

Last Call This business advised its customers to pick up suits and gowns. The sign tells customers that the owner will not take suits to Owens Valley, California, where the Manzanar Camp was located.

Clearance Japanese Americans had to close what were flourishing businesses, settling for whatever they could sell in a hurry. ▶

Closed Overnight, businesses shut their doors as their owners had to report to relocation centers.

▲

Japanese Americans packed up and moved within a matter of weeks. Armed guards supervised the evacuation and gave advice to evacuees.

from

Desert Exile

BY YOSHIKO UCHIDA

The Civilian Exclusion Order instructed Japanese-American families to take only what they could carry. This set off a wave of fire sales, in which the families sold most of their possessions at deeply discounted prices. Most families had only ten days to prepare for evacuation. The well-known writer Yoshiko Uchida was in her last year at the University of California, Berkeley, when Pearl Harbor was attacked. Her father was arrested later that day. In April, 1942, the Uchida family was interned at Tanforan Assembly Center. In her memoir Desert Exile: The Uprooting of a Japanese American Family, *Uchida described the turmoil of packing up and selling off.*

It was one of those rare Sundays when we had no guests for dinner. My parents, sister, and I had just come home from church and were having a quiet lunch when we heard a frenzied voice on the radio break in on the program. The Japanese had attacked Pearl Harbor.

"Oh no," Mama cried out. "It can't be true."

"Of course not," Papa reassured her. "And if it is, it's only the work of a fanatic."

We all agreed with him. Of course it could only be an **aberrant**[1] act of some crazy irresponsible fool. It never for a moment occurred to any of us that this meant war. As a matter of fact, I was more concerned about my approaching finals at the university than I was with this bizarre news and went to the library to study. When I got there, I found clusters of Nisei students anxiously discussing the shocking event. But we all agreed it was only a freak incident and turned our attention to our books. I stayed at the library until 5:00 P.M. giving no further thought to the attack on Pearl Harbor.

When I got home, the house was filled with an uneasy quiet. A strange man sat in our living room and my father was gone. The FBI had come to pick him up, as they had dozens of other Japanese men. Executives of Japanese business firms, shipping lines, and banks, men active in local Japanese associations, teachers of Japanese language schools, virtually every leader of the Japanese American community along the West Coast had been seized almost immediately.

Actually the FBI had come to our house twice, once in the absence of my parents and sister who, still not realizing the serious nature of the attack, had gone out to visit friends. Their absence, I suppose, had been cause for suspicion and the FBI or police had broken in to search our house without a warrant. On returning, my father, believing that we had been burglarized, immediately called the police. Two policemen appeared promptly with three FBI men and suggested that my father check to see if his valuables were missing. They were, of course, undisturbed, but their location was thereby revealed. Two of the FBI men requested that my father accompany them "for a short while" to be questioned, and my father went willingly. The other FBI

---

[1] **aberrant**—deviating from the norm; unusual.

man remained with my mother and sister to intercept all phone calls and to inform anyone who called that they were indisposed.

One policeman stationed himself at the front door and the other at the rear. When two of our white friends came to see how we were, they were not permitted to enter or speak to my mother and sister, who, for all practical purposes, were prisoners in our home.

By the time I came home, only one FBI man remained but I was alarmed at the startling turn of events during my absence. In spite of her own anxiety, Mama in her usual thoughtful way was serving tea to the FBI agent. He tried to be friendly and courteous, reassuring me that my father would return safely in due time. But I couldn't share my mother's gracious attitude toward him. Papa was gone, and his abrupt custody into the hands of the FBI seemed an ominous **portent**[2] of worse things to come. I had no inclination to have tea with one of its agents, and went abruptly to my room, slamming the door shut.

Eventually, after a call from headquarters, the FBI agent left, and Mama, Kay, and I were alone at last. Mama made supper and we sat down to eat, but no one was hungry. Without Papa things just weren't the same, and none of us dared voice the fear that sat like a heavy black stone inside each of us.

"Let's leave the porch light on and the screen door unlatched," Mama said hopefully. "Maybe Papa will be back later tonight."

But the next morning the light was still burning, and we had no idea of his whereabouts. All that day and for three days that followed, we had no knowledge of what had happened to my father. And somehow during those days, I struggled through my finals.

---

[2] **portent**—omen.

It wasn't until the morning of the fifth day that one of the men apprehended with my father, but released because he was an American citizen, called to tell us that my father was being detained with about one hundred other Japanese men at the Immigration Detention Quarters in San Francisco. The following day a postcard arrived from Papa telling us where he was and asking us to send him his shaving kit and some clean clothes. "Don't worry, I'm all right," he wrote, but all we knew for certain was that he was alive and still in San Francisco.

As soon as permission was granted, we went to visit him at the Immigration Detention Quarters, a drab, dreary institutional structure. We went in, anxious and **apprehensive**,[3] and were told to wait in a small room while my father was summoned from another part of the building. As I stepped to the door and looked down the dingy hallway, I saw Papa coming toward me with a uniformed guard following close behind. His steps were eager, but he looked worn and tired.

"Papa! Are you all right?"

He hugged each of us.

"I'm all right. I'm fine," he reassured us.

But our joy in seeing him was short-lived, for he told us that he was among a group of ninety men who would be transferred soon to an army internment camp in Missoula, Montana.

"Montana!" we exclaimed. "But we won't be able to see you anymore then."

"I know," Papa said, "but you can write me letters and I'll write you too. Write often, and be very careful—all of you. Kay and Yo, you girls take good care of Mama." His concern was more for us than for himself.

When it was time to say goodbye, none of us could speak for the ache in our hearts. My sister and I began to cry. And it was Mama who was the strong one.

---

[3] **apprehensive**—worried; troubled; distressed.

The three of us watched Papa go down the dark hallway with the guard and disappear around a corner. He was gone, and we didn't know if we would ever see him again. There were rumors that men such as my father were to be held as hostages in **reprisal**[4] for atrocities committed by the Japanese soldiers. If the Japanese killed American prisoners, it was possible my father might be among those killed in reprisal.

It was the first time in our lives that Papa had been separated from us against his will. We returned home in silent gloom, my sister dabbing at her eyes and blowing her nose as she drove us back to Berkeley. When we got home, we comforted ourselves by immediately packing and shipping a carton of warm clothing to Papa in Montana, glad for the opportunity to do something to help him.

As soon as our friends heard that my father had been interned, they gathered around to give us support and comfort, and for several days running we had over fifteen callers a day.

Upon reaching Montana, my father wrote immediately, his major concern being whether we would have enough money for our daily needs. He and my mother were now classified as "enemy aliens" and his bank account had been blocked immediately. For weeks there was total confusion regarding the amount that could be withdrawn from such blocked accounts for living expenses, and early reports indicated it would be only $100 a month.

"Withdraw as much as you can from my account," Papa wrote to us. "I don't want you girls to dip into your own savings accounts unless absolutely necessary."

As the oldest citizen of our household, my sister now had to assume responsibility for managing our business affairs, and it was not an easy task. There were

---

[4] **reprisal**—an act of retaliation or an attempt to pay back someone for a wrong.

many important papers and documents we needed, but the FBI had confiscated all of my father's keys, including those to his safe deposit box, and their inaccessibility was a problem for us.

We exchanged a flurry of letters as my father tried to send detailed instructions on how to endorse checks on his behalf; how to withdraw money from his accounts; when and how to pay the premiums on his car and life insurance policies; what to do about filing his income tax returns which he could not prepare without his records; and later, when funds were available, how to purchase defense bonds for him. Another time he asked us to send him a check for a fellow internee who needed a loan.

My father had always managed the business affairs of our household, and my mother, sister, and I were totally unprepared to cope with such tasks. Our confusion and bewilderment were overwhelming, and we could sense my father's frustration and anguish at being unable to help us except through censored letters, and later through internee telegrams which were permitted to discourage letter-writing. Papa's letters were always in English, not only for the benefit of the censor, but for my sister and me. And we could tell from each one that he was carefully reviewing in his mind every aspect of our lives in Berkeley.

"Don't forget to lubricate the car," he would write. "And be sure to prune the roses in January. Brush Laddie every day and give him a pat for me. Don't forget to send a monthly check to Grandma and take my Christmas offering to church."

In every letter he reassured us about his health, sent greetings to his friends, and expressed concern about members of our church.

"Tell those friends at church whose businesses have been closed not to be discouraged," he wrote in one of his first letters. "Tell them things will get better before long."

And he asked often about his garden.

From the early days of my father's detention, there had been talk of a review board that would hold hearings to determine whether and when each man would be released. Although Papa's letters were never discouraging in other respects, he cautioned us not to be optimistic whenever he wrote of the hearings. We all assumed it would be a long, slow process that might require months or even years.

It developed that hearings for each of the interned men were to be conducted by a Board of Review comprised of the district attorney, representatives of the FBI, and immigration authorities of the area in which the men had formerly resided. The recommendation of the review board plus papers and **affidavits**[5] of support were to be sent to Washington for a final decision by the attorney general. As soon as we learned of this procedure, we asked several of our white friends to send affidavits verifying my father's loyalty to the United States and supporting his early release. They all responded immediately, eager to do anything they could to help him.

The interned men did not dare hope for early release, but they were anxious to have the hearings over with. As they were called in for their interviews, some were photographed full-face only, while others were photographed in profile as well, and it was immediately rumored that those photographed twice would be detained as hostages. Two of the questions they were asked at the interview were, "Which country do you think will win the war?" and "If you had a gun in your hands, at whom would you shoot, the Americans or the Japanese?" In reply to the second question, most answered they would have to shoot straight up.

In accordance with Army policy, the men were never informed of plans in advance and were moved

---

[5] **affidavits**—sworn statements or testimonies.

before they became too familiar with one installation. One morning half the men in my father's barrack were summoned, told that they were being shipped to another camp, and stripped of everything but the clothes on their backs. They were then loaded onto buses, with only a few minutes to say goodbye to their friends. Their destination was unknown. . . .

The first mass removal of the Japanese began in Terminal Island, a fishing community near San Pedro, and because these people were close to a naval base, their treatment was harsh. With most of their men already interned as my father was, the remaining families had to cope with a three-day deadline to get out of their homes. In frantic haste they were forced to sell their houses, businesses, and property. Many were exploited cruelly and suffered great financial losses.

We knew it was simply a matter of time before we would be notified to evacuate Berkeley as well. A five-mile travel limit and an 8:00 P.M. curfew had already been imposed on all Japanese Americans since March, and enemy aliens were required to register and obtain identification cards. Radios with short wave, cameras, binoculars, and firearms were designated as "contraband" and had to be turned in to the police. Obediently adhering to all regulations, we even brought our box cameras to the Berkeley police station where they remained for the duration of the war.

We were told by the military that "voluntary evacuation" to areas outside the West Coast restricted zone could be made before the final notice for each sector was issued. The move was hardly "voluntary" as the Army labeled it, and most Japanese had neither the funds to leave nor a feasible destination. The three of us also considered leaving "voluntarily," but like the others, we had no one to go to outside the restricted zone.

Some of our friends warned us to consider what life would be like for three women in a "government assembly center" and urged us to go anywhere in order to remain free. On the other hand, there were those who told us of the arrests, violence, and vigilantism encountered by some who had fled "voluntarily." Either decision would have been easier had my father been with us, but without him both seemed fraught with uncertainties.

In Montana my father, too, was worried about our safety. He wrote us of an incident in Sacramento where men had gained entrance to a Japanese home by posing as FBI agents and then attacked the mother and daughter. "Please be very careful," he urged. We decided, finally, to go to the government camp where we would be with friends and presumably safe from violence. We also hoped my father's release might be facilitated if he could join us under government custody.

Each day we watched the papers for the evacuation orders covering the Berkeley area. On April 21, the headlines read: "Japs Given Evacuation Orders Here." I felt numb as I read the front page story. "Moving swiftly, without any advance notice, the Western Defense Command today ordered Berkeley's estimated 1,319 Japanese, aliens and citizens alike, evacuated to the Tanforan Assembly Center by noon, May 1." (This gave us exactly ten days' notice.) "Evacuees will report at the Civil Control Station being set up in Pilgrim Hall of the First Congregational Church . . . between the hours of 8:00 A.M. and 5:00 P.M. next Saturday and Sunday."

This was Exclusion Order Number Nineteen, which was to uproot us from our homes and send us into the Tanforan Assembly Center in San Bruno, a hastily converted racetrack.

All Japanese were required to register before the departure date, and my sister, as head of the family, went to register for us. She came home with baggage and name tags that were to bear our family number and be attached to all our belongings. From that day on we became Family Number 13453.

Although we had been preparing for the evacuation orders, still when they were actually issued, it was a sickening shock.

"Ten days! We have only ten days to get ready!" my sister said frantically. Each day she rushed about, not only taking care of our business affairs, but, as our only driver, searching for old crates and cartons for packing, and taking my mother on various errands as well.

Mama still couldn't seem to believe that we would have to leave. "How can we clear out in ten days a house we've lived in for fifteen years?" she asked sadly.

But my sister and I had no answers for her.

Mama had always been a saver, and she had a tremendous accumulation of possessions. Her frugal upbringing had caused her to save string, wrapping paper, bags, jars, boxes, even bits of silk thread left over from sewing, which were tied end to end and rolled up into a silk ball. Tucked away in the corners of her desk and bureau drawers were such things as small stuffed animals, wooden toys, *kokeshi* dolls, marbles, and even a half-finished pair of socks she was knitting for a teddy bear's paw. Many of these were "found objects" that the child in her couldn't bear to discard, but they often proved useful in providing diversion for some fidgety visiting child. These were the simple things to dispose of.

More difficult were the boxes that contained old letters from her family and friends, our old report cards from the first grade on, dozens of albums of family photographs, notebooks and sketch pads full of our childish drawings, valentines and Christmas cards we had made for our parents, innumerable guest books filled with the signatures and friendly words of those who had once been entertained. These were the things my mother couldn't bear to throw away. Because we didn't own our house, we could leave nothing behind. We had to clear the house completely, and everything in it had either to be packed for storage or thrown out.

We surveyed with desperation the vast array of dishes, lacquerware, silverware, pots and pans, books, paintings, porcelain and pottery, furniture, linens, rugs, records, curtains, garden tools, cleaning equipment, and clothing that filled our house. We put up a sign in our window reading, "Living room sofa and chair for sale." We sold things we should have kept and packed away foolish trifles we should have discarded. We sold our refrigerator, our dining room set, two sofas, an easy chair, and a brand new vacuum cleaner with attachments. Without a sensible scheme in our heads, and lacking the practical judgment of my father, the three of us packed frantically and sold recklessly. Although the young people of our church did what they could to help us, we felt desperate as the deadline approached. Our only thought was to get the house emptied in time, for we knew the Army would not wait.

Organizations such as the First Congregational Church of Berkeley were extremely helpful in anticipating the needs of the panic-stricken Japanese and provided immediate, practical assistance. Families of the church offered storage space to those who needed it, and we took several pieces of furniture to be stored in the basement of one such home. Another non-Japanese friend offered to take our books and stored more than eight large cartons for us. In typical Japanese fashion, my mother took gifts to express her gratitude to each person who helped us.

Our two neighboring families, one Swiss and the other Norwegian, were equally helpful. We had grown up with the two blond Norwegian girls, whose ages nearly matched my sister's and mine. We had played everything from "house" to "cops and robbers" with them and had spent many hot summer afternoons happily sipping their father's home-made root beer with them.

The two boys in the Swiss family were younger, and I had taken one of them to grammar school every day when he was in kindergarten. In loving admiration, he had offered to marry me when he grew up. We were close to our neighbors and they both extended the warmth of their friendship to us in those hectic days. We left our piano and a few pieces of furniture with one, and we piled all the miscellaneous objects that remained on the last day into the garage of the other.

The objects too large to leave with friends, such as beds, mattresses and springs, extra quilts, and rugs, we stored in a commercial storage house, whose monthly statements never failed to reach us even in the stalls of Tanforan or, later, in the sandy wastes of Utah.

Not knowing what crude inadequate communal facilities we might have in camp, we also took the precaution of getting typhoid shots and lost a day of packing, which we could ill afford, as we nursed sore arms and aching heads.

Two problems that remained unsolved until very near our departure deadline were what to do with Laddie, our pet collie, and our almost new Buick sedan. A business associate of my father's offered to store the car in his garage for us, but a few months after we entered Tanforan he needed the space and sold it for us for $600.

Our pedigreed Scotch collie was a gentle friendly dog, but our friends didn't want to take him because of his age. In desperation, I sent a letter to our university's student newspaper, the *Daily Californian.*

I am one of the Japanese American students soon to be evacuated and have a male Scotch collie that can't come with me. Can anyone give him a home? If interested, please call me immediately at Berkeley 7646W.

I was quickly deluged with calls, one of which was from a fraternity that wanted a mascot. But we decided on the first boy who called because he seemed kind and genuinely concerned.

"I'll pay you for him," he offered, trying to be helpful.

But how could we accept money for our old family pet? We eventually gave the boy everything that belonged to Laddie, including his doghouse, leash, food bowl, and brushes.

It was a particularly sad day for my sister, who was the avid animal-lover of our family. It was she who had begged, cajoled, and coerced my parents into getting all of our dogs. But once they became our pets, we all loved them, and Mama used to cook a separate pot of vegetables to feed our dogs along with their cans of Dr. Ross's dog food.

Although the new owner of our pet had promised faithfully to write us in camp, we never heard from him. When, finally, we had a friend investigate for us, we learned that the boy hadn't the heart to write us that Laddie had died only a few weeks after we left Berkeley. . . .

Our bedrooms were now barren except for three old mattresses on which we slept until the day we left. But in one corner of my mother's room there was an enormous shapeless canvas blanket bag which we called our "camp bundle." Into its flexible and obliging depths we tossed anything that wouldn't fit into the two suitcases we each planned to take. We had been instructed to take only what we could carry, so from time to time we would have a practice run, trying to see if we could walk while carrying two full suitcases.

Having given us these directions, the Army with its own peculiar logic also instructed us to bring our bedding, dishes, and eating utensils. Obviously the only place for these bulky items was in the "camp bundle." Into it we packed our blankets, pillows, towels, rubber boots, a tea kettle, a hot plate, dishes and silverware, umbrellas, and anything else that wouldn't fit in our suitcases. As May 1 drew near, it grew to gigantic and cumbersome proportions, and by no stretch of our imagination could we picture ourselves staggering into camp with it.

"Mama, what'll we ever do with that enormous thing?" my sister worried.

"We obviously can't carry that thing on our backs," I observed.

But all Mama could say was, "I'm sure things will work out somehow."

There was nothing to be done but to go on filling it and hope for the best. In the meantime, we watched uneasily as it continued to grow, bulging in all directions like some wild living thing.

We could have been spared our anxiety and agonizing had we known trucks would be available to transport our baggage to camp. But it is entirely possible the omission of this information in our instructions was intentional to discourage us from taking too much baggage with us.

The night before we left, our Swiss neighbors invited us to dinner. It was a fine feast served with our neighbors' best linens, china, and silverware. With touching concern they did their best to make our last evening in Berkeley as pleasant as possible.

I sat on the piano bench that had been in our home until a few days before and thought of the times I had sat on it when we entertained our many guests. Now, because of the alarming succession of events that even then seemed unreal, I had become a guest myself in our neighbors' home.

When we returned to our dark empty house, our Norwegian neighbors came to say goodbye. The two girls brought gifts for each of us and hugged us goodbye.

"Come back soon," they said as they left.

But none of us knew when we would ever be back. We lay down on our mattresses and tried to sleep, knowing it was our last night in our house on Stuart Street.

Neat and conscientious to the end, my mother wanted to leave our house in perfect condition. That last morning she swept the entire place, her footsteps echoing sadly throughout the vacant house. Our Swiss neighbors brought us a cheering breakfast on bright-colored dishes and then drove us to the First Congregational Church designated as the Civil Control Station where we were to report.

We were too tense and exhausted to fully sense the terrible wrench of leaving our home, and when we arrived at the church, we said our goodbyes quickly. I didn't even turn back to wave, for we were quickly absorbed into the large crowd of Japanese that had already gathered on the church grounds.

It wasn't until I saw the armed guards standing at each doorway, their bayonets mounted and ready, that I realized the full horror of the situation. Then my knees sagged, my stomach began to churn, and I very nearly lost my breakfast.

Hundreds of Japanese Americans were crowded into the great hall of the church and the sound of their voices pressed close around me. Old people sat quietly, waiting with patience and resignation for whatever was to come. Mothers tried to comfort crying infants, young children ran about the room, and some teenagers tried to put up a brave front by making a social opportunity of the occasion. The women of the church were serving tea and sandwiches, but very few of us had any inclination to eat.

Before long, we were told to board the buses that lined the street outside, and the people living nearby came out of their houses to watch the beginning of our strange migration. Most of them probably watched with curious and **morbid**[6] fascination, some perhaps even with a little sadness. But many may have been relieved and glad to see us go.

Mama, Kay, and I climbed onto one of the buses and it began its one-way journey down familiar streets we had traveled so often in our own car. We crossed the Bay Bridge, went on beyond San Francisco, and sped down the Bayshore Highway. Some of the people on the bus talked nervously, one or two wept, but most sat quietly, keeping their thoughts to themselves and their eyes on the window, as familiar landmarks slipped away one by one.

As we rode down the highway, the grandstand of the Tanforan racetrack gradually came into view, and I could see a high barbed wire fence surrounding the entire area, pierced at regular intervals by tall guard towers. This was to be our temporary home until the government could construct inland camps far removed from the West Coast.

The bus made a sharp turn and swung slowly onto the racetrack grounds. As I looked out the window for a better view, I saw armed guards close and bar the barbed wire gates behind us. We were in the Tanforan Assembly Center now and there was no turning back.

---

[6] **morbid**—mentally unhealthy; characterized by gloomy or unwholesome ideas.

QUESTIONS TO CONSIDER

1. In what ways were the legal rights of Japanese Americans violated?

2. How did neighbors and community members react to the impending internment of Japanese Americans?

3. What emotions do you think were felt by the people on the bus as they headed for Tanforan Assembly Center?

from

Snow Falling on Cedars

BY DAVID GUTERSON

David Guterson's award-winning novel Snow Falling on Cedars
*(1994) revolves around the events on San Piedro Island, in the
Puget Sound off the coast of Washington state, in 1941. In flash-
backs from 1950, Guterson describes how the internment of the
Japanese Americans ripped the island apart. One of his characters
is Hatsue, a Japanese-American teenager with a white boyfriend.
In the excerpt below, Guterson describes what was happening to
Hatsue's family and her bewilderment about her identity and future.*

Two weeks later, on February 4, a black Ford
threaded through the Imadas' fields, making for the
house of cedar slats. Hatsue was standing at the verge of
the woodshed, filling her apron with cedar kindling
from a pile underneath a sheet of waxed canvas, when
she noticed—this was odd—that the Ford's headlights
had been blackened; she heard the car before she saw it.

It came to a halt just in front of her house; two men emerged in suits and ties. They shut their doors gently and looked at each other; one of them straightened his coat a little—he was bigger than the other, and his sleeves were not long enough to cover even half of his shirt cuffs. Hatsue stood silently with her apron full of kindling while the men mounted the porch and knocked on the door, holding their hats in their hands. Her father answered in his sweater and sandals, his newspaper dangling from his left hand neatly and his reading glasses perched on the bridge of his nose; her mother stood just behind him.

"Allow me to introduce myself," said the smaller of the men, producing a badge from his coat pocket. "Federal Bureau of Investigation," he announced. "Are you He-say-o Imada?"

"Yes," said Hatsue's father. "Is something wrong?"

"Not wrong exactly," said the FBI man. "It's just that we've been asked to search this place. You understand, we're going to search. Now if you'll just step inside, please, we'll all sit down."

"Yes, come in," said Hatsue's father.

Hatsue dropped her apron full of kindling back onto the pile of cedar sticks. The two men turned to look at her; the larger one came halfway down the porch steps. Hatsue walked out of the shadow of the wood-shed and into the glow of the porch light. "You come in, too," said the smaller man.

They crowded into the living room. While Hatsue and her sisters sat on the couch, Hisao brought chairs from the kitchen for the FBI men—the larger one followed him everywhere. "Please, sit down," offered Hisao.

"You're real polite," replied the smaller man. Then he took an envelope from his coat pocket; he handed it over to Hisao. "It's a warrant from the U.S. district attorney. We're going to search the premises—it's an order, see, an order."

Hisao held the envelope between his fingers but made no move to open it. "We are loyal," he said. That was all.

"I know, I know," said the FBI man. "Still, we've got to look around."

While he spoke the larger man stood and shot his cuffs, then calmly opened Fujiko's glass case and picked up the stack of *shakuhachi* [Japanese flute] sheet music she kept on the bottom shelf. He picked up Fujiko's bamboo flute, turned it over twice in his hands—small hands for such a thick, cloddish man—then set it on the dining room table. There was a magazine stand beside the wood stove, and he pawed through the magazines there. He picked up Hisao's newspaper.

"We've had some complaints from local citizens that certain enemy aliens on San Piedro Island have in their possession items declared illegal **contraband**,"[1] said the smaller man. "It's our job to search the premises for these. We ask for your cooperation."

"Yes, of course," said Hisao.

The larger man went into the kitchen. They could see him through the doorway peering beneath the sink and opening the oven door. "We're going to have to search through your private effects," the small FBI man explained. He stood and took the envelope from Hisao; he put it back in his coat pocket. "I hope you won't mind," he added.

He opened the *tansu*—a chest of drawers in one corner of the living room. He took out Fujiko's silk kimono with its gold brocaded sash. "That's very nice," he said, holding it to the light. "From the old country, it appears. High class."

---

[1] **contraband**—prohibited goods or merchandise.

The larger man came through the living room from the pantry with Hisao's shotgun seized in one hand and four boxes of shells against his chest. "The guy's all armed," he said to his partner. "There's a big old sword back there, too."

"Put it all on the table," said the small man. "And tag everything, Wilson—did you bring the tags in?"

"They're in my pocket," Wilson answered.

The youngest of the Imada girls began to whimper, covering her face with her hands. "Hey, little girl," said the FBI man. "I know this is kind of scary—but guess what? There's nothing to cry about, you hear me? We'll be done and out of your way soon."

The large man, Wilson, went back for Hisao's sword. Then he turned his attention to the bedrooms.

"Tell you what," said the first man to Hisao. "Let's just sit tight until Wilson is finished. Then you and me, we'll take a walk outside. We'll tag these things up and load them in the car. Then you can show me around your outbuildings. We have to check everything—that's the way it is."

"I understand," said Hisao. He and Fujiko were holding hands now.

"Don't be nervous," said the FBI man. "We'll be out of your hair in a few minutes."

He stood at the table putting tags on things. For a while he waited in silence. He tapped his foot and put his mouth to the flute. "Wilson!" he said finally. "Get your paws off the underwear!" Then he chuckled and picked up Hisao's shotgun.

"We gotta take this," he said apologetically. "All this stuff, you understand. They'll hold it for a while—who knows why?—then they'll ship it all back to you. They'll ship it back when they're done with it. It's complicated, but that's the way it is. There's a war on and that's the way it is."

"The flute is precious," said Hisao. "The kimono, the sheet music—you must take those things?"

"Anything like that, yeah," said the FBI man. "Any old-country stuff we have to take."

Hisao was silent, his brow furrowed. Wilson came back from the bedrooms looking solemn; he carried Hatsue's scrapbook. "Pervert," said his partner. "Come on."

"Crap," said Wilson. "I was going through the drawers. You do it next time if you don't like it."

"He-say-o and I are going out," the small man said firmly. "You can sit here with the ladies and finish up with these tags. And be polite," he added.

"I'm always polite," said Wilson.

Hisao and the small man went outside; Wilson worked on the tags. When he was done he browsed through Hatsue's scrapbook, chewing on his bottom lip. "Strawberry Princess," he said, looking up. "You must 'a' been flattered by that."

Hatsue didn't answer. "It's a good picture," added Wilson. "It looks like you. Looks just like you, in fact."

Hatsue said nothing. She wished Wilson would get his hands off her scrapbook. She was thinking of asking him, politely, to put it down, when Hisao and the other man came through the door, the FBI man carrying a crate. "Dynamite," he said. "Look at this, Wilson." He set the crate lightly on the table. The two men stood pawing through the dynamite—twenty-four sticks of it. Wilson chewed on his cheek and stared.

"You must believe me," insisted Hisao. "This is for tree stumps, for clearing land."

The smaller FBI man shook his head gravely. "Maybe," he said. "But this is still bad. This stuff"—he pointed a finger at the crate—"this is illegal contraband. You were supposed to have turned this stuff in."

They took the gun, the shells, the sword, and the dynamite and put it all in the car trunk. Wilson came back with a duffel bag and stuffed in the scrapbook, the kimono, the sheet music, and finally the bamboo flute.

When everything was loaded in the trunk of their car the FBI men sat down again. "Well," said the smaller one. "This is it. Guess what?" he said to Hisao.

Hisao didn't answer. He sat in his sandals and sweater blinking, holding his glasses in his hand: He waited for the FBI man to speak.

"We gotta arrest you," said Wilson. "You're going on a trip to Seattle." He unhooked a pair of handcuffs from his belt; they were clipped on next to his gun.

"You don't need those," urged the smaller man. "This guy here is a class act, a gentleman. There's no need for any handcuffs." He turned his attention to Hisao. "They're just going to ask you some questions, okay? We go down to Seattle, a few questions, a few answers, the whole thing is over."

The two younger girls were both crying. The youngest buried her face in her hands, and Hatsue put an arm around her. She pulled her sister's head in close and stroked her hair gently. Hisao rose from his chair.

"Please not take him," said Fujiko. "He has done no bad things. He—"

"Nobody knows about that," said Wilson. "There's nobody who can say."

"Probably in just a few days," said the other man. "These things take a little time, you see. We have to take him on down to Seattle. He's gotta be scheduled in and all. Maybe a few days, maybe a week."

"A week?" said Fujiko. "But what we do? What do you—"

"Think of it as a war sacrifice," the FBI man interrupted. "Figure to yourself there's a war on, you see, and everybody's making some sacrifices. Maybe you could look at it that way."

Hisao asked if he could change out of his sandals and get his coat from the pantry. He wanted to pack a small bag, he added, if that would be acceptable. "Both," said Wilson. "Go ahead. We're perfectly willing to accommodate."

They allowed him to kiss his wife and daughters and to say good-bye to each. "Call Robert Nishi," Hisao told them. "Tell him I am arrested." But when Fujiko called it turned out that Robert Nishi had been arrested as well. Ronald Kobayashi, Richard Sumida, Saburo Oda, Taro Kato, Junkoh Kitano, Kenzi Yamamoto, John Masui, Robert Nishi—they were all in a Seattle jail now. They had all been arrested on the same night.

The arrested men rode on a train with boarded windows—prisoners had been shot at from railroad sidings—from Seattle to a work camp in Montana. Hisao wrote a letter to his family each day; the food, he said, was not very good, but they were not really being mistreated. They were digging trenches for a water system that would double the size of the camp. Hisao had gotten a job in the laundry ironing and folding clothes. Robert Nishi worked in the camp kitchen.

Hatsue's mother gathered her five daughters together, Hisao's letters in her hand. She told her daughters, once again, the story of her odyssey from Japan on board the *Korea Maru*. She told them about the Seattle rooms she had cleaned, the sheets on which white men had vomited blood, the toilets full of their excrement, the stench of their alcohol and sweat. She told them about the waterfront cookhouse where she'd worked chopping onions and frying potatoes for *hakujin* stevedores[2] who looked right through her as if she weren't even there. She knew, already, about hardship, she said her life had long been difficult. She knew what it was to be alive without being alive; she knew what it was to be invisible. She wanted her daughters to know how to face this in a manner that would allow them

---

[2] stevedores—people who work at loading and unloading ships in port.

their dignity. Hatsue sat motionless while her mother spoke, trying to guess at her meaning. She was eighteen now, and her mother's story held more weight than it had when she'd heard it earlier. She leaned forward and listened carefully. Her mother predicted that the war with Japan would force all her daughters to decide who they were and then to become more Japanese. Wasn't it true that the *hakujin* didn't really want them in their country? There were rumors that all the Japanese on the coast were going to be forced to leave. There was no point in trying to conceal anything or in trying to pretend they were not Japanese—the *hakujin* could see it in their faces; they were going to have to accept this. They were Japanese girls in America during a time when America was fighting a war with Japan—did any of them want to deny it? The trick was to live here without hating yourself because around you was hatred. The trick was to refuse to allow your pain to prevent you from living honorably. In Japan, she said, a person learned not to complain or be distracted by suffering. To **persevere**[3] was always a reflection of the state of one's inner life, one's philosophy, and one's perspective. It was best to accept old age, death, injustice, hardship—all of these were part of living. Only a foolish girl would deny this was so, thus revealing to the world her immaturity and the degree to which she lived in the world of the *hakujin* instead of in the world of her own people. And her people, insisted Fujiko, were Japanese—the events of the past months had proved it so; why else had their father been arrested? The events of the last two months should teach them something about the darkness in the hearts of the *hakujin* and the more general darkness that was part of living. To deny that there was this dark side to life would be like pretending that the cold of winter was somehow only a temporary

---

[3] **persevere**—to persist in spite of opposition or discouragement.

illusion, a way station on the way to the higher "reality" of long, warm, pleasant summers. But summer, it turned out, was no more real than the snow that melted in wintertime. Well, said Fujiko, now, your father is gone, folding laundry in a camp in Montana, and we all must get by, endure. "Do you understand?" she said in Japanese. "There is no choice in the matter. We will all have to endure."

"They don't all hate us," Hatsue replied. "You're exaggerating, mother—you know you are. They're not so different from us, you know. Some hate, others don't. It isn't all of them."

"I know what you're saying," said Fujiko. "Not all of them hate—you're correct. But on this other matter"—she still spoke in Japanese—"you don't think they are very much different? In some big way, Hatsue? Different from us?"

"No," said Hatsue. "I don't."

"They are," said Fujiko, "and I can tell you how. The whites, you see, are tempted by their egos[4] and have no means to resist. We Japanese, on the other hand, *know* our egos are nothing. We bend our egos, all of the time, and that is where we differ. That is the fundamental difference, Hatsue. We bend our heads, we bow and are silent, because we understand that by ourselves, alone, we are nothing at all, dust in a strong wind, while the *hakujin* believes his aloneness is everything, his separateness is the foundation of his existence. He seeks and grasps, seeks and grasps for his separateness, while we seek union with the Greater Life—you must see that these are distinct paths we are traveling, Hatsue, the *hakujin* and we Japanese."

"These people seeking union with the Greater Life," argued Hatsue, "are the ones who bombed Pearl Harbor. If they're so ready to bend and bow, then what

---

[4] egos—plural of *ego*, or the self (as contrasted to another self or the world).

are they doing attacking all over the world and taking over other countries? I don't feel I'm a part of them," said Hatsue. "I'm a part of *here*," she added. "I'm from this place."

"Yes, you were born here, that's so," said Fujiko "But your blood—you are still Japanese."

"I don't want to be!" said Hatsue. "I don't want anything to do with them! Do you hear me? I don't want to be Japanese!"

Fujiko nodded at her eldest daughter. "These are difficult times," she replied. "Nobody knows who they are now. Everything is cloudy and unclear. Still, you should learn to say nothing that will cause you regret. You should not say what is not in your heart—or what is only in your heart for a moment. But you know this— silence is better."

Hatsue knew immediately that her mother was right. Her mother, clearly, was serene and unruffled, and her voice carried the strength of truth. Hatsue fell silent, ashamed of herself. Who was she to say how she felt? What she felt remained a mystery, she felt a thousand things at once, she could not unravel the thread of her feelings with enough certainty to speak with any accuracy. Her mother was right, silence was better. It was something—one thing—she knew with clarity.

"I could say" her mother went on, "that living among the *hakujin* has tainted you, made your soul impure, Hatsue. This lack of purity envelops you—I see it every day. You carry it with you always. It is like a mist around your soul, and it haunts your face like a shadow at moments when you do not protect it well. I see it in your eagerness to leave here and walk in the woods in the afternoon. I cannot translate all of this easily, except as the impurity that comes with living each day among the white people. I am not asking you to shun them entirely—this you should not do. You must live in this world, of course you must, and this world is the world of the *hakujin*—you must learn to live in it, you must go to school. But don't allow living *among* the *hakujin* to become living *intertwined* with them. Your soul will decay. Something fundamental will rot and go sour. You are eighteen, you are grown now—I can't walk with you where you are going anymore. You walk alone soon, Hatsue. I hope you will carry your purity with you always and remember the truth of who you are."

QUESTIONS TO CONSIDER

1. What do you think the FBI man means when he says, "It's complicated, but that's the way it is. There's a war on and that's the way it is"?

2. Why did Hatsue's mother gather her and her sisters to tell them again about her own difficult odyssey from Japan to America? What was her point in retelling her children this story?

3. What does Hatsue's mother mean when she says to her, "I hope you will carry your purity with you always and remember the truth of who you are"?

Poetry: The Evacuation Order

Dwight Okita and Mitsuye Yamada are Japanese Americans whose parents were interned during World War II. The poems "In Response to Executive Order 9066" and "Warning" are attempts to imagine what it was like for Japanese Americans during the evacuation and internment. Both poems are full of irony. Okita speaks in the voice of his mother, who was a young girl when the family was interned, while Yamada adopts the voice of a young woman who has tried to assimilate.

In Response to Executive Order 9066

BY DWIGHT OKITA

Dear Sirs:
Of course I'll come. I've packed my galoshes
and three packets of tomato seeds. Denise calls them
love apples. My father says where we're going
they won't grow.

I am a fourteen-year-old girl with bad spelling
and a messy room. If it helps any, I will tell you
I have always felt funny using chopsticks
and my favorite food is hot dogs.
My best friend is a white girl named Denise—
we look at boys together. She sat in front of me
all through grade school because of our names:
O'Connor, Ozawa. I know the back of Denise's
   head very well.
I tell her she's going bald. She tells me I copy on tests.
We're best friends.

I saw Denise today in Geography class.
She was sitting on the other side of the room.
"You're trying to start a war," she said "giving
   secrets
away to the Enemy, Why can't you keep your big
mouth shut?"

I didn't know what to say.
I gave her a packet of tomato seeds
and asked her to plant them for me, told her
when the first tomato ripened
she'd miss me.

Warning

BY MITSUYE YAMADA

The voice of my father came to me
from a corner of his cell
(marked Dangerous Enemy Alien)

Do not sign your legal name
to anything not
on petitions for any cause
in the street
at meetings or rallies
not on receipts for orders,
special deliveries or C.O.D.s

I was my father's daughter
I had followed his advice assiduously
never left my thumbprints anywhere
never gave my stamp of approval
to anything
never cast my soulprint in cement
never raised my voice on billboards
and one day disappeared anyway
behind barbed wires.
They put up a sign on buildings
telephone poles and store fronts:
For all persons who never left a mark.

"My silences had not protected me."

QUESTIONS TO CONSIDER

1. How would you describe the tone of Okita's letter?

2. What is the significance of the tomato seeds mentioned in
   the first and last paragraphs of Okita's letter?

3. What does Yamada's poem suggest about the lasting effects
   the internment had on Japanese Americans?

Families Relocate

To Owens Valley A mother and daughter wait at a train
station for the train that will evacuate them from the West
Coast to Owens Valley.

Buses Families were evacuated by bus to the Tanforan Assembly Center. Here a family from Hayward, California, prepares to move.

Here boys wait at Santa Fe Station for a train to take them to Owens Valley.
▼

Checking In The head of this Japanese family checks in at an assembly center before being evacuated to a War Relocation Center.

Ready to Move Japanese-American families cooperated with U.S. authorities. The evacuation occurred in a peaceful and orderly fashion.

▼

▲
Under Guard Even though Japanese Americans cooperated with authorities, their evacuation was supervised by armed guards.

Trains Trains transported many Japanese Americans to new locations further inland.

▲

Moving Families Here families of Japanese ancestry are being kept together and bused to a Relocation Center.

After arriving at assembly centers by train, people waited to board buses to take them to their final destinations. ▶

Trucks Trucks also served as a form of transportation. They were jammed with suitcases, blankets, household goods, and children.

Life in the Camps

from

Nisei[1] Daughter

BY MONICA SONE

*Once Japanese-American families had sold off their possessions
and reported to the control centers, they were bused to temporary
camps known as "assembly centers." These were generally converted
fairgrounds, stockyards, or racetracks and offered neither enough
space nor sanitary facilities for the thousands of families being
interned. Monica Sone was the child of Japanese immigrants. She
was born in Washington state in 1919 and had graduated from
business school before the war started. In 1953, Sone published*
Nisei Daughter, *a memoir of growing up Japanese American and
a record of what had happened to her during the war. In the
following selection, Sone describes how her family coped with the
nightmare of packing up and being put in "Camp Harmony," an
assembly center at Puyallup, Washington.*

Everyone was dressed casually, each according to
his idea of where he would be going. One Issei[2] was
wearing a thick mackinaw jacket and cleated, high-

---

[1] Nisei—the first generation of ethnic Japanese born in the United States.

[2] Issei—the immigrant generation from Japan.

topped hiking boots. I stared admiringly at one hand-some couple, standing slim and poised in their ski clothes. They looked newly wed. They stood holding hands beside their streamlined luggage that matched smartly with the new Mr. and Mrs. look. With an air of resigned sacrifice, some Issei women wore dark-colored slacks with deep-hemmed cuffs. One gnarled old grand-mother wore an ankle-length black crepe dress with a plastic initial "S" pinned to its high neckline. It was old-fashioned, but dignified and womanly.

Automobiles rolled up to the curb, one after another, discharging more Japanese and more baggage. Finally at ten o'clock, a vanguard of Greyhound busses purred in and parked themselves neatly along the curb. The crowd stirred and murmured. The bus doors opened and from each, a soldier with rifle in hand stepped out and stood stiffly at attention by the door. The murmur-ing died. It was the first time I had seen a rifle at such close range and I felt uncomfortable. This rifle was presumably to quell riots, but contrarily, I felt riotous emotion mounting in my breast.

Jim Shigeno, one of the leaders of the Japanese-American Citizens' League, stepped briskly up front and started reading off family numbers to fill the first bus. Our number came up and we pushed our way out of the crowd. Jim said, "Step right in." We bumped into each other in nervous haste. I glanced nervously at the soldier and his rifle, and I was startled to see that he was but a young man, pink-cheeked, his clear gray eyes staring impassively ahead. I felt that the occasion prob-ably held for him a sort of tense anxiety as it did for us. Henry found a seat by a window and hung out, watching for Minnie who had promised to see him off. Sumi and I suddenly turned maternal and hovered over Mother and Father to see that they were comfortably settled. They were silent.

Newspaper photographers with flash-bulb cameras pushed busily through the crowd. One of them rushed up to our bus, and asked a young couple and their little boy to step out and stand by the door for a shot. They were reluctant, but the photographers were persistent and at length they got out of the bus and posed, grinning widely to cover their embarrassment. We saw the picture in the newspaper shortly after and the caption underneath it read, "Japs good-natured about evacuation."

Our bus quickly filled to capacity. All eyes were fixed up front, waiting. The guard stepped inside, sat by the door, and nodded curtly to the gray-uniformed bus driver. The door closed with a low hiss. We were now the Wartime Civil Control Administration's babies.

When all the busses were filled with the first contingent of Japanese, they started creeping forward slowly. We looked out of the window, smiled and feebly waved our hands at the crowd of friends who would be following us within the next two days. From among the Japanese faces, I picked out the tall, spare figures of our young people's minister, the Reverend Everett Thompson, and the Reverend Emery Andrews of the Japanese Baptist Church. They were old friends, having been with us for many years. They wore bright smiles on their faces and waved vigorously as if to lift our morale. But Miss Mahon, the principal of our Bailey Gatzert Grammar School and a much-beloved figure in our community, stood in front of the quiet crowd of Japanese and wept openly.

Sumi suddenly spied Minnie, driving her family car. The car screeched to a halt and Minnie leaped out, looking frantically for Henry. Henry flung his window up and shouted, "Minnie! Minnie! Over here!" The bystanders, suddenly good-humored, directed her to our moving bus. Minnie ran up to the windows, puffing, "Sorry I was late, Henry! Here, flowers for you."

She thrust a bouquet of fresh yellow daffodils into his outstretched hand. Henry shouted, "Thanks—I'll be seeing you, I hope."

When our bus turned a corner and we no longer had to smile and wave, we settled back gravely in our seats. Everyone was quiet except for a chattering group of university students who soon started singing college songs. A few people turned and glared at them, which only served to increase the volume of their singing. Then suddenly a baby's sharp cry rose indignantly above the hubbub. The singing stopped immediately, followed by a guilty silence. Three seats behind us, a young mother held a wailing red-faced infant in her arms, bouncing it up and down. Its angry little face emerged from multiple layers of kimonos, sweaters and blankets, and it, too, wore the white pasteboard tag pinned to its blanket. A young man stammered out an apology as the mother gave him a **wrathful**[3] look. She hunted frantically for a bottle of milk in a shopping bag, and we all relaxed when she had found it.

We sped out of the city southward along beautiful stretches of farmland, with dark, newly turned soil. In the beginning we devoured every bit of scenery which flashed past our window and admired the massive-muscled work horses plodding along the edge of the highway, the rich burnished copper color of a browsing herd of cattle, the vivid spring green of the pastures, but eventually the sameness of the country landscape palled on us. We tried to sleep to escape from the restless anxiety which kept bobbing up to the surface of our minds. I awoke with a start when the bus filled with excited buzzing. A small group of straw-hatted Japanese farmers stood by the highway, waving at us. I felt a sudden warmth toward them, then a twinge of pity. They would be joining us soon.

---

[3] **wrathful**—filled with anger or indignation.

About noon we crept into a small town. Someone said, "Looks like Puyallup, all right." Parents of small children babbled excitedly, "Stand up quickly and look over there. See all the chick-chicks and fat little piggies?" One little city boy stared hard at the hogs and said tersely, "They're *bachi*—dirty! "

Our bus idled a moment at the traffic signal and we noticed at the left of us an entire block filled with neat rows of low shacks, resembling chicken houses. Someone commented on it with awe, "Just look at those chicken houses. They sure go in for poultry in a big way here." Slowly the bus made a left turn, drove through a wire-fenced gate, and to our dismay, we were inside the oversized chicken farm. The bus driver opened the door, the guard stepped out and stationed himself at the door again. Jim, the young man who had shepherded us into the busses, popped his head inside and sang out, "Okay, folks, all off at Yokohama, Puyallup."

We stumbled out, stunned, dragging our bundles after us. It must have rained hard the night before in Puyallup, for we sank ankle deep into gray, **glutinous**[4] mud. The receptionist, a white man, instructed us courteously, "Now, folks, please stay together as family units and line up. You'll be assigned your apartment."

We were standing in Area A, the mammoth parking lot of the state fairgrounds. There were three other separate areas, B, C and D, all built on the fair grounds proper, near the baseball field and the race tracks. This camp of army barracks was hopefully called Camp Harmony.

We were assigned to apartment 2-1-A, right across from the bachelor quarters. The apartments resembled elongated, low stables about two blocks long. Our home was one room, about 18 by 20 feet, the size of a living room. There was one small window in the wall opposite

---

[4] **glutinous**—gummy, having the quality of glue.

the one door. It was bare except for a small, tinny wood-burning stove crouching in the center. The flooring consisted of two by fours laid directly on the earth, and dandelions were already pushing their way up through the cracks. Mother was delighted when she saw their shaggy yellow heads. "Don't anyone pick them. I'm going to cultivate them."

Father snorted, "Cultivate them! If we don't watch out, those things will be growing out of our hair."

Just then Henry stomped inside, bringing the rest of our baggage. "What's all the excitement about?"

Sumi replied **laconically**,[5] "Dandelions."

Henry tore off a fistful. Mother scolded, "*Arra! Arra!* Stop that. They're the only beautiful things around here. We could have a garden right in here."

"Are you joking, Mama?"

I chided Henry, "Of course, she's not. After all, she has to have some inspiration to write poems, you know, with all the '*nali keli's.*' I can think of a poem myself right now:

Oh, Dandelion, Dandelion,
Despised and uprooted by all,
Dance and bob your golden heads
For you've finally found your home
With your yellow fellows, *nali keli*, amen!"

Henry said, thrusting the dandelions in Mother's black hair, "I think you can do ten times better than that, Mama."

Sumi reclined on her seabag and fretted, "Where do we sleep? Not on the floor, I hope."

"Stop worrying," Henry replied disgustedly.

Mother and Father wandered out to see what the other folks were doing and they found people wandering

---

[5] **laconically**—using a minimum of words.

in the mud, wondering what other folks were doing. Mother returned shortly, her face lit up in an ecstatic smile, "We're in luck. The latrine is right nearby. We won't have to walk blocks."

We laughed, marveling at Mother who could be so poetic and yet so practical. Father came back, bent double like a woodcutter in a fairy tale, with stacks of scrap lumber over his shoulder. His coat and trouser pockets bulged with nails. Father dumped his loot in a corner and explained, "There was a pile of wood left by the carpenters and hundreds of nails scattered loose. Everybody was picking them up, and I hustled right in with them. Now maybe we can live in style with tables and chairs."

The block leader knocked at our door and announced lunchtime. He instructed us to take our meal at the nearest mess hall. As I untied my seabag to get out my pie plate, tin cup, spoon and fork, I realized I was hungry. At the mess hall we found a long line of people. Children darted in and out of the line, skiing in the slithery mud. The young stood impatiently on one foot, then the other, and scowled, "The food had better be good after all this wait." But the Issei stood quietly, arms folded, saying very little. A light drizzle began to fall, coating bare black heads with tiny sparkling raindrops. The chow line inched forward.

Lunch consisted of two canned sausages, one lob of boiled potato, and a slab of bread. Our family had to split up, for the hall was too crowded for us to sit together. I wandered up and down the aisles, back and forth along the crowded tables and benches, looking for a few inches to squeeze into. A small Issei woman finished her meal, stood up and hoisted her legs modestly over the bench, leaving a space for one. Even as I thrust myself into the breach, the space had shrunk to two inches, but I worked myself into it. My dinner companion, hooked just inside my right elbow, was a bald headed, gruff-looking Issei man who seemed to resent nestling at mealtime. Under my left elbow was a tiny, mud-spattered girl. With busy runny nose, she was belaboring her sausages, tearing them into shreds and mixing them into the potato gruel which she had made with water. I choked my food down.

We cheered loudly when trucks rolled by, distributing canvas army cots for the young and hardy, and steel cots for the older folks. Henry directed the arrangement of the cots. Father and Mother were to occupy the corner nearest the wood stove. In the other corner, Henry arranged two cots in L shape and announced that this was the combination living room-bedroom area, to be occupied by Sumi and myself. He fixed a male den for himself in the corner nearest the door. If I had had my way, I would have arranged everyone's cots in one neat row as in Father's hotel dormitory.

We felt fortunate to be assigned to a room at the end of the barracks because we had just one neighbor to worry about. The partition wall separating the rooms was only seven feet high with an opening of four feet at the top, so at night, Mrs. Funai next door could tell when Sumi was still sitting up in bed in the dark, putting her hair up. "*Mah*, Sumi-*chan*," Mrs. Funai would say through the plank wall, "are you curling your hair tonight again? Do you put it up every night?" Sumi would put her hands on her hips and glare defiantly at the wall.

The block monitor, an impressive Nisei who looked like a star tackle with his crouching walk, came around the first night to tell us that we must all be inside our room by nine o'clock every night. At ten o'clock, he rapped at the door again, yelling, "Lights out!" and Mother rushed to turn the light off not a second later.

Throughout the barracks, there were a medley of creaking cots, whimpering infants and explosive night coughs. Our attention was riveted on the intense little wood stove which glowed so violently I feared it would melt right down to the floor. We soon learned that this condition lasted for only a short time, after which it suddenly turned into a deep freeze. Henry and Father took turns at the stove to produce the harrowing blast which all but singed our army blankets, but did not penetrate through them. As it grew quieter in the barracks, I could hear the light patter of rain. Soon I felt the "splat! splat!" of raindrops digging holes into my face. The dampness on my pillow spread like a mortal bleeding, and I finally had to get out and haul my cot toward the center of the room. In a short while Henry was up. "I've got multiple leaks, too. Have to complain to the landlord first thing in the morning."

All through the night I heard people getting up, dragging cots around. I stared at our little window, unable to sleep. I was glad Mother had put up a makeshift curtain on the window for I noticed a powerful beam of light sweeping across it every few seconds. The lights came from high towers placed around the camp where guards with Tommy guns[6] kept a twenty-four-hour vigil. I remembered the wire fence encircling us, and a knot of anger tightened in my breast. What was I doing behind a fence like a criminal? If there were accusations to be made, why hadn't I been given a fair trial? Maybe I wasn't considered an American anymore. My citizenship wasn't real, after all. Then what was I? I was certainly not a citizen of Japan as my parents were. On second thought, even Father and Mother were more alien residents of the United States than Japanese nationals for they had little tie with their mother country. In their twenty-five years in America, they had worked and paid their taxes to their adopted government as any other citizen.

---

[6] Tommy guns—submachine guns.

Of one thing I was sure. The wire fence was real. I no longer had the right to walk out of it. It was because I had Japanese ancestors. It was also because some people had little faith in the ideas and ideals of democracy. They said that after all these were but words and could not possibly insure loyalty. New laws and camps were surer devices. I finally buried my face in my pillow to wipe out burning thoughts and snatch what sleep I could.

QUESTIONS TO CONSIDER

1. Why did her mother want to cultivate the dandelions once they reached Camp Harmony?

2. What were the conditions in the barracks like? How might those conditions have affected the Nisei interned there?

from

Citizen 13660

BY MINÉ OKUBO

*From the assembly centers, guarded trains took the Japanese
Americans to one of the ten newly constructed internment camps:
Topaz in Utah, Poston and Gila River in Arizona, Ameche in
Colorado, Jerome and Rohwer in Arkansas, Minidoka in Idaho,
Manzanar and Tule Lake in California, and Heart Mountain in
Wyoming. Most of these camps were in remote areas, where escape
was unthinkable. Camp life was highly regimented, but the internees
quickly adapted and made the best of their situation, starting
newspapers, schools, and creating a social life. Miné Okubo (1912–)
worked as an art director for the Topaz newspaper. This eventually
led to her release when in 1944* Fortune *magazine offered
her a job, which allowed her to leave Topaz. Okubo published her
drawings of Topaz camp life in* Citizen 13660 *(1946).*

I had always wanted to come out East, but I didn't
know anybody and I was shy. So when the evacuation
came, I said, "God has answered my prayers!" All my
friends asked why don't I go East instead of going to
camp. I said, "No, I'm going camping!"

At the time I was working for the WPA doing art-work—murals in mosaic and **fresco**[1] for the army in Oakland. I was working in the daytime when Pearl Harbor was bombed. We were taken completely by surprise, but we thought the citizens wouldn't be evacuated.

There was a curfew from 8 P.M. to 6 A.M. I had to get a special permit from the government so I could go beyond the five-mile radius to go to Oakland for work. I worked and finished the murals a few days before the evacuation day.

My mother had died before evacuation, so my youngest brother came to live with me in Berkeley. Another brother was drafted in the army before Pearl Harbor. My father was living alone in Riverside. My sister came from Pomona to visit him one day and the whole house had been ransacked—everything we had, all the old Japanese suitcases filled with parents' old kimonos, my parents' past life. Everything had been stolen. Everything. It looked like he had been taking a bath and cooking when the FBI came to take him away. My sister made inquiries and found him in the Riverside jail. But they wouldn't let her see him. You see, anyone who was connected with any Japanese organization was considered potentially dangerous and when Mother died, Father started helping at the Japanese church. He was shipped to a [U.S. Department of Justice] camp in Missoula, Montana.

My brother and I were evacuated to Tanforan race-track for six months and then to Topaz, Utah, for one and one-half years. I would get letters from my father. It would read: "Dear Miné, Block, block, block" [blocked out by the censor] and his name signed. So I never found out what happened. Then I received letters from Louisiana. It was the same: block, block, block, block. Finally I had a letter from him saying they were releasing

---

[1] **fresco**—a mural painting on damp plaster.

him. That was while I was still in camp. They had cleared him. He decided to go to Heart Mountain to be with my sister and brother. But before evacuation he had met a widow in the Japanese church and she was in the Poston camp. Father was very lonely so I told him he should transfer. He did go there and they were finally married and eventually moved back to Japan. He died there.

In Tanforan, before we went to Utah, all those that had any business problems that they wanted to settle could get out for one day, with a guard. This poor fellow went out of his mind! I took him to the University of California. Met all the professors. And fed him at the faculty club. Bought lots of candy; we weren't allowed candies at that time. We just made it back to camp in time. It was crazy. I mean if you were guilty or something, fine. But it's a strange feeling to have a guard along. But everything was insane when you didn't do anything. All these people—young babies, pregnant mothers—how can they be dangerous? The whole thing is so outlandish that you can't believe it.

Tanforan was awful. My brother and I didn't have proper clothing or equipment—just had a whisk broom to sweep out all the manure and dust in our stable. The smell! We cleaned the stall, stole lumber, and turned our stall into a home. Adapt and adjust right away, that's my whole nature.

You could hear all the people crying, the people grinding their teeth; you could hear everything. Even lovemaking. It turned out that the barrack that my brother and I were in was a special stable for young married couples. Later on this neighbor came quietly to me and said we ought to move because we weren't married. I said, "If there's any moving to be done, it's going to be you because we're all settled." But everything ended well. We were never home.

I was always busy. In the daytime I went around sketching. There wasn't any photographing allowed so I decided to record everything. Observing. I went around doing all these minute sketches of people and events. I didn't sleep much.

I worked all night at the newspaper. It was lunacy to work all night, going twenty-four hours a day. I was art editor for the daily newspaper and art editor for *Trek* literary magazine.

I made many friends in camp. Those working on the newspaper and many others. With ten thousand people in a mile-square area, everybody knew everybody. There were many interesting people. I was considered quite a character. There was absolutely no privacy, so I nailed up a **quarantine**[2] sign to discourage visitors. I would say I had hoof and mouth disease. I still have the sign. You have to live the camp life to know what it was like.

When visitors came, they had to stand in the middle of the highway. And all the cars would go by and they would yell, "You Jap lovers!" So I discouraged my friends from coming.

In Topaz the barracks were better—clean except for the alkali powder dust. We stole right away all the lumber and things. Those that came late didn't have anything. We went out at night, falling into ditches and pipes. It was just chaos. Deep ditches with humps of dirt because they were still building the camp. It was dark as the ace of spades with no lights anywhere. It was quite an experience.

They had hobby shows in camp, very well received. Everybody in camp displayed their talents. They made use of everything in camp. Rocks, pebbles, fruit wrapping, seeds, cardboard, fence, anything they could find. Clever, beautiful, interesting. I did a huge collage using

---

[2] **quarantine**—a period of enforced seclusion, usually to prevent the spread of disease.

rolls of toilet paper. They didn't know what to make of it. Gave many a good laugh though!

I taught art in camp to children. I liked the children and students. It is a two-way learning—we learn from each other. Each one is an individual and needs individual attention. It was interesting. I remember the girls drew pictures about camp and camp life. The boys were more imaginative. Their pictures were on war, airplanes, circus, and subjects out of camp.

But for the children, camp wasn't too bad. Children can take anything. Everything was a circus to them. But it was hard on the old people and mothers with children. Children attracted children and they would run off to play.

In camp I kept myself busy. I knew what I wanted to do. All my friends on the outside were sending me extra food and crazy gifts to cheer me up. Once I got a box with a whole bunch of worms even. So I decided I would do something for them. I started a series of drawings telling them the story of my camp life. At the time I wasn't thinking of a book; I was thinking of an exhibition, but these drawings later became my book *Citizen 13660*. So I just kept a record of everything, objective and humorous, without saying much so they could see it all. Humor is the only thing that mellows life, shows life as the circus it is.

After being uprooted, everything seemed ridiculous, insane, and stupid. There we were in an unfinished camp, with snow and cold. The evacuees helped sheetrock the walls for warmth and built the barbed wire fence to fence themselves in. We had to sing "God Bless America" many times with a flag. Guards all around with shot guns, you're not going to walk out. I mean . . . what could you do? So many crazy things happened in the camp. So the joke and humor I saw in the camp was not in a joyful sense, but ridiculous and insane. It was dealing with people and situations. The humor was always, "It is fate. It can't be helped. What's going to happen next?" I tried to make the best of it, just adapt and adjust.

Like growing up in Riverside, California. We were poor, so I got used to living by my wits. My oldest brother, like Robin Hood, attracted all the rebellious and lost. They were good people, very idealistic, but off the main road. Children, young people, adults gathered in our backyard every day: at night fifty, sixty people around a bonfire telling stories—ghost stories, crime stories, fairy tales. There were all kinds of sports and games—boxing and wrestling. It was great fun. I was just a shy little girl watching. Very shy, but very observing and wanting to know everything. If anybody talked to me, I would run to the next block!

In our family my mother and father were real disappointed because all the children were independent-minded. We listened but we would not follow. None of us would go to Japanese school, so we talked mixed-up Japanese and English. They were disappointed to think that everyone's children were becoming doctors and dentists and all of their children were complete monkeys, I mean real birds on the creative side. Well, of course, Mama and Papa were both creative too. She was a good artist and a calligrapher, and he was a scholar. But Mama encouraged me from the beginning. I used to follow her around with paints and brushes. . . . That's my beginning.

I'm coming from parents who suffered so much and were so persecuted. I had already seen life. I always observed. Even at that time, I saw how you are basically an individual and different, and society is trying to make you the same, so it can control you. So, being off the main road, I decided I'm always going to have some trouble.

I am not bitter. Evacuation had been a great experience for me because I love people and my interest is people. It gave me the chance to study human beings from cradle to grave, when they were all reduced to one status. And I could study what happens to people. At the beginning they were all together—comradeship and humor—but as camp grew, they started becoming status conscious, bettering their homes, being better than Mr. Jones. Just like what happens in the establishment. People are people; everywhere it's the same. Only the backdrop and stage is different. Just have to change the scenery. People have the same concerns for home, family, comfort, security, and loads of problems. That's all there is when you come to think of it.

So how people reacted to the evacuation depends. There are different personal reactions to everything. Disaster always brings change both good and bad. Certain people get bitter, **vengeful**.[3] I am a creative, aware person. Like I said before, an observer and reporter. I am recording what happens, so others can see and so this may not happen to others.

I was planning on staying in camp; I didn't have any money and at least I was being fed! Then I got a telegram from *Fortune* magazine. I had always thought that if you are patient enough, the gods would answer your prayers. So I left for New York. I had my belongings in great big crates sent to *Fortune* magazine, since I had no other address. They had no idea what to do with all my things. There was no room in their ancient little cubby-hole office. During the war it was next to impossible to find a place to live in New York, but they all went out looking for places for me.

One woman from the magazine saw my camp ink and rice paper sketches and suggested I write a book. It was so difficult getting it published. At that time anything Japanese was still rat poison. Columbia University Press saw the value of my story and printed

---

[3] **vengeful**—seeking revenge; spiteful.

it in 1946. Gradually, interest developed and my drawings were exhibited all over the United States. But it was really too soon after the war. Anything Japanese was a touchy subject.

So I went into commercial art and did everything from soup to nuts. But it took me ten years to realize that commercial art was just an establishment game, not what I wanted. I'm an individual who wants to contribute to the betterment of this world. To me, life and art are one and the same. It took me forty years to find this out, but now I have arrived. The key is simplifying. I deal with the highest value of vision: what reality is and what it is not. I only simplify the content of reality into my own imaginative writing. By mastering drawing, color and craft, I express the content of reality—that which is universal and timeless. It's a long, lonely road, but there's no other way. In my next life, maybe I'll come back as a Japanese beetle!

QUESTIONS TO CONSIDER

1. What character traits helped Okubo endure the hardships of the camps?

2. Why did Okubo say that the humor she saw in the camp was "not in a joyful sense, but ridiculous and insane"?

3. What lessons about life did Okubo learn from her experience in the camp?

4. In what sense is Okubo's art an important historical artifact?

from

Lone Heart Mountain

BY ESTELLE ISHIGO

Estelle Ishigo was a Caucasian married to a Japanese American. She worked as an artist and teacher in California. In 1942, she chose to be evacuated and interned with her husband rather than be separated. Fiercely opposed to this outrage, Ishigo used her talents to record the life forced on Japanese Americans by the U.S. government. She wrote and illustrated her memoir Lone Heart Mountain *while still incarcerated in the Heart Mountain camp. The book was one of the strongest protests against the treatment of Japanese Americans. The following is a selection from Ishigo's account of camp life and a portfolio of her stirring images.*

When slanting spears of light pierced the grey stillness of a camp uncovered from the deep winter snow; when the icebound earth gave way and softened—then came a half-awakening memory.

In the rafters, above an army cot, came a chorus of chirpings from newly-hatched sparrows, filling a young boy's dreams with visions of mulberry trees, great leafy boughs flecked with sunlight dancing through green shades, and the chittering of birds. The boy held this enchanting vision, reluctant to leave it for the life that was NOW!

The clang of pounding iron, mess hall doors and sound of heavy boots on barrack floors brought back in focus the drab walls of the room and the long black rows of barracks in the grey sage-covered wasteland.

Day by day the sun crept higher, the earth grew softer and dust rose again into the air. We were now permitted by the "Authority" to step outside the gate.

On application several passes were given each day to visit a neighboring town, stating destination, time of departure and return. The townspeople objected to too many of us being there at one time. A numbered identification button was issued at the gate lest someone might not return, although there was no question of running away. There was no place to run away to.

There was little money to spend in town, but the pleasure of being permitted to ride down the highway in a bus, to walk on sidewalks, look in store windows and see how people lived outside, was a welcome relief despite being told by drivers sometimes to sit by ourselves in the rear.

Now an old one would walk along the fence, sometimes lifting the wire and slowly wandering, hermit-like out into the barren wilderness. The river we had been told about long ago was found; but to go there without a pass was forbidden.

A mile and a half away the waters of the Shoshone River wandered around hillocks and cliffs and drew thirsty willows to its banks, murmuring the promise of a way of life and peace to any who found his way there, creeping unobserved by guards through a tunnel of irrigation pipe. In this manner the joyous **communion**[1] with the living river, the beaver and salamander, the birds and insects living in the willowed growth, and all the life that joined in its song, was one's own—private. A God given communion. Some chose the pipe route rather than apply for permission for a pass from the "Authority" with its "TIME TO GO" and "TIME TO RETURN. . . ."

From within this prison community (now the second largest in the state of Wyoming) the "Authority" picked a supervisor to organize youth clubs under competent leaders. The camp was divided into zones and many clubs were formed to direct work and play under supervised leadership. To harness young rebellious spirits into constructive cooperation was the plan of the War Relocation Authority—for the home was gone—the cord of parental guidance broken. There were separate clubs for boys and girls, divided into five sections with a supervisor for each section. Each club was required to submit a list of members, officers and its constitution for approval of the "Authority" and later some were given Y.M.C.A. and Y.W.C.A. charters. In the dull **monotony**[2] and restriction of this prison-like camp, the young folks were permitted to have dances and holiday socials. Here the crude severity of the barracks dominated the environment and the mess hall; rooms were required to be lighted by four uncovered light globes and all affairs to be over by twelve midnight.

A police department was formed and headquarters set up in the office building of the "Authority." A station with trucks and uniformed men was established in one of the camp barracks. Policemen were picked from among us although there was little need for services of

[1] **communion**—intimate connection marked by a sense of harmony and kinship.

[2] **monotony**—tedious sameness.

such among the camp population. One night an emergency wartime blackout drill was ordered in this far away wild and lonely place.

On Sundays hundreds of men, women and young people dressed in their best. With necktie and polished shoes, parasol, ribbons and high heels they hiked over the rutted roads and gullies through dust and mud to go to church services. These were held in separate barracks—Christian, Catholic, Salvation Army, Seventh Day Adventist and Buddhist.

Some spent Sundays the same as any other day. It was a long distance to the laundry room to fill a bucket for watering only a seed, but with great **perseverance**[3] a poetic interpretation of nature was seen in the skill of arranging rocks and wild native growth. An old bachelor caught horned toads and kept them in a box in his room—feeding them from a jar of ants. Some caught birds and tamed them for companionship. Every animal was a potential friend except snakes and the crows that cast shadows as they soared and circled above the camp.

A library was started in an empty barrack. Girl Scouts sent out for donations of books and magazines for the few shelves. There were chairs and tables and books lay stacked on the floor. A building for High School was erected in the center of the camp with a library and auditorium to be used for a gymnasium. Commencement exercises were held here with a school band playing "Pomp and Circumstance" as the graduates marched in solemn procession with heads bowed during the benediction and hope in their hearts for a better future.

The English classes had the largest attendance. Classes were held on Americanization—American History—Current Social Problems and Trends for the

---

[3] **perseverance**—persistence in spite of opposition or discouragement.

Japanese American, as well as Social Science—with consideration of democracy and the role of the individual. There was instruction in the history, development, ideals and principles of cooperative and application of cooperative techniques. Shorthand and secretarial training was available especially for project secretaries. Mathematics, a general introduction to physical and biological sciences, writing and techniques of the drama—with emphasis upon the dramatic interpretation of assembly centers and evacuation experiences. There were classes for the development of leadership for the community; agriculture, arts and crafts and teacher training. Caucasian teachers served as heads of each department. Eventually a few teachers of Japanese ancestry were permitted to serve under them. Over a thousand people enrolled.

"Authority" personnel discovered there was considerable talent among the camp population and permitted those who had been in the theatrical profession to organize Japanese drama groups. Some of the costumes and musical instruments were made in camp and some were sent for from storage in the warehouses. Whatever scrap material could be found was used to make backdrops and scenery of old Japan. Young people who had studied the arts of their parents, performed with music and dance.

It was strictly forbidden to speak Japanese or perform any type of Japanese culture on the stage of the High School building, so crude platforms were set up at one end of a mess hall and here the beautiful, ancient dramas, music and dancing of old Japan were performed.

The performers came in costumes from dressing rooms in the nearest barracks; musicians came with samisen, koto, shakuhachi[4] and drums. The Heart Mountain Mandolin Band with its dancers and singers

---

[4] samisen, koto, shakuhachi—Japanese instruments.

entertained and sometimes the Takuragawa and Hawaiian band played for us. They came in summer sandstorms and winter blizzards every few weeks, touring mess halls throughout the camp and we sat spellbound while the color and sound momentarily transformed our environment. These entertainers donated their time and work for the people's enjoyment. They were not employed by the "Authority."

Occasionally, some members of the audience, according to an old Japanese custom, would send a small envelope with a little money back stage to the performer. The envelope would wish the performer "Good Luck" printed in bright red Japanese letters. After a time, the Community Activity Department requested that such tokens of appreciation received by performers be turned over to them as all entertainment was under the jurisdiction of Community Activity which, in turn, was part of the Camp Cooperative System.

Artists were interned here, too. A list of names of those who wished to continue painting and form an Art Student League was submitted with a program recommending this as a necessity and of public interest. There was a continued appeal from this group for a barrack where they might continue their work and study. Many lived in crowded rooms of bachelors or with large families. This request was met with disapproval by "'Authority" who stated that art was not considered a necessity or necessarily of public interest. With continued appeal from the artists, "Authority" finally allowed them temporarily one half of a barrack for the study of drawing and painting—if it promised to be "educational." Within a short time an exhibit was held in this barrack of paintings and carvings and proved to be of great interest to the community. Yet this group continued to be unrecognized as a worthy activity for almost a year until some artists agreed to help in the poster shop when an order came for 4,000 silk screen posters for the Navy Department in Washington. Only then did their work receive acknowledgment from "Authority" as a worthy activity for public interest.

QUESTIONS TO CONSIDER

1. Why does Ishigo feel that the relocation camps helped break up homes and families?

2. What artistic pleasures or relief does Ishigo mention that helped make the internment somewhat bearable?

Drawings by
Estelle Ishigo

Estelle Ishigo

We are Americans, again?

"Shikata Ga Nai"

BY JOHN SANFORD

John Sanford's book The Winters of That Country *is a book of vignettes that examine important incidents in American history. Vignettes are short literary descriptions, which try to be pictures in words. "Shikata Ga Nai" is a Japanese proverb which means "What happened, happened." Sanford uses it as the title for a vignette that presents a picture of the internment of Japanese Americans.*

They wore tags, all of them, a narrow strip of cardboard hanging from a button by a string, and coming along a street somewhere, or plodding across a bridge, they might've been goods in motion, a procession of merchandise offering itself for sale. The elderly, as in a will-less dream, drifted with the flow of the young, and toylike children were buoyant on the stream. Passing before the curious at the wayside, they might've been wares on display, a showing of faces, fashions, but only the children stared back at blue-eyed staring.

The ticketed people were on their way to **banishment**,[1] but not beyond the pale of their country: their place of exile lay within it, at an inner confine called Topaz, Tule, Manzanar, and they were moving now toward its towns in the desert, toward league-long reaches of mesquite[2] and ocotillo,[3] toward shimmering **scrims**[4] of heat and winds that were made of dust. They were headed for trains of **passé**[5] cars, days and nights of empty views, for a compound called Minidoka, Gila, Heart Mountain, deep inside the compound land. Their tar-paper mansions waited under the sun, black ovens, and they'd sleep in wet-down sheets and bleed from the nose in the heat. Infants would wilt and die, and blistered by blown sand, families and friends would bury them among the creosote[6] bushes, and on a stone some day one would be known as Jerry.

It would not be long before the old ones sat gazing off into the distance as if there were nothing near they cared to see. They'd look out across scrub and sage at a dim sierra, a wedgwood band at the base of the sky. They'd sit quite still in the midst of movement, they'd be unaware of the roundabout commotion, hear none of the cries and collisions, none of the running feet, and not a word would be heard of the traffic on the air. They'd be somewhere in the far blue mountains: their past, the best of life, was there.

The young, if they dreamt at all, would dream at night: their days would hold no bygone vistas. There'd be shacks to mend, doors that didn't fit, cracks in the shrunken floors. Who would moon over blue **buttes**[7]

---

[1] **banishment**—driven away; expulsion.

[2] mesquite—a spiny tree or shrub.

[3] ocotillo—a thorny scarlet-flowered shrub.

[4] **scrims**—transparent curtains.

[5] **passé**—outdated.

[6] creosote—a desert shrub.

[7] **buttes**—isolated hills with steep sides and small summits.

and pompous clouds when there were snakes to roust and centipedes? There'd be winds to deal with and force-fed dust, there'd be the range of the seasons, the mile-high heat and cold, there'd be barrens to claim, sand-burs to burn, thistle, arrowgrass, and there'd be a need to learn and wait.

The price-tagged children in doll-size clothes wouldn't know that watch-towers weren't trees. They'd suppose they simply grew as they'd grown, with ladders instead of branches and lamps instead of leaves. Nor would they know that warnings were on the walls, signs on the wire, **tethers**[8] on their perfect feet. They'd play, shrill, sit in the sand and seem to think, they'd chatter at the soldiers and never know they were guards who'd kill. They'd never be afraid, never be sad, bereft, abused, and yet one day (shikata ga nai) they'd begin to hate: what happened would happen to them.

---

[8] **tethers**—ropes or chains that limit one's range of movement.

QUESTIONS TO CONSIDER

1. Other than the physical afflictions, what hardships were endured by the Japanese Americans interned in the southwest?

2. What is the significance of the Japanese saying "Shikata Ga Nai"?

3. In what way were interned Japanese Americans dehumanized?

Poetry: Internment Camps

Internees had no choice but to create a regular life for themselves in the camps. Schools had to be run and the Wartime Relocation Authority provided work for all who wanted it. Newspapers and magazines appeared in the camps, choirs were formed, and clubs sprang up. The resilience of the Japanese Americans showed through quickly as they built furniture and did what they could to make life bearable. Writing poetry is one of Japan's most ancient and respected arts, and many internees turned to poetry to record their experiences. Some poetry was written for the newspapers and magazines, but most was simply a personal expression. The following is a grouping of poems written in the internment camps. The poems depict the dismay of life in a prison.

That Damned Fence

ANONYMOUS

They've sunk in posts deep into the ground,
They've strung wires all the way around.
With machine gun nests just over there,
And **sentries**[1] and soldiers everywhere!

We're trapped like rats in a wired cage
To fret and fume with **impotent**[2] rage;
Yonder whispers the lure of the night
But that D A M N E D   F E N C E **assails**[3] our sight.

We seek the softness of the midnight air,
But that D A M N E D   F E N C E in the floodlight glare
Awakens unrest in our **nocturnal**[4] quest,
And mockingly laughs with vicious jest.

With nowhere to go and nothing to do,
We feel terrible, lonesome, and blue;
That D A M N E D   F E N C E is driving us crazy,
Destroying our youth and making us lazy.

Imprisoned in here for a long, long time,
We know we're punished though we've committed
   no crime
Our thoughts are gloomy and enthusiasm damp,
To be locked up in a concentration camp.

---

[1] **sentries**—guards.

[2] **impotent**—lacking strength or power.

[3] **assails**—attacks.

[4] **nocturnal**—relating to or occurring in the night.

Loyalty we know and patriotism we feel,
To sacrifice our utmost was our ideal.
To fight for our country, and die, mayhap;
Yet we're here because we happen to be a Jap.

We all love life, and our country best,
Our misfortune's to be here in the west;
To keep us penned behind that DAMNED FENCE
Is someone's notion of National Defense!!!

My Mom, Pop, and Me

BY ITSUKO TANIGUCHI

My Mom, Pop, & me
Us living three
Dreaded the day
When we rode away,
Away to the land
With lots of sand
My mom, pop, & me.

The day of evacuation
We left our little station
Leaving our friends
And my tree that bends
Away to the land
With lots of sand
My mom, pop, & me.

Manzanar

BY MICHIKO MIZUMOTO

Dust storms.
Sweat days.
Yellow people,
Exiles.
I am the mountain that kisses the sky in the dawning.
I watched the day when these, your people, came into
    your heart.
        Tired.
        Bewildered.
        Embittered.

I saw you accept them compassion, **impassive**[5] but
    visible.
Life of a thousand teemed within your bosom.
Silently you received and bore them.
        Daily you fed them from your breast,
        Nightly you soothed them to forgetful slumber,
Guardian and keeper of the unwanted.

They say your people are **wanton**[6]
        Saboteurs.
        Haters of white men.
        Spies.
Yet I have seen them go forth to die for their only
    country,
Help with the defense of their homeland,
America.

---

[5] **impassive**—unmoved; free of emotion.

[6] **wanton**—wild or reckless; unrestrained.

I have seen them look with beautiful eyes at nature.
And know the **pathos**[7] of their tearful laughter,
Choked with enveloping mists of the dust storms,
Pant with the heat of sweat-days; still laughing.
    Exiles.

And I say to these you **harbor**[8] and those on the exterior,
Scoff[9] if you must, but the dawn is approaching,
When these, who have learned and suffered in silent
  courage;
Better, wiser, for the unforgettable interlude of
  detention,
Shall trod on free sod again,
Side by side peacefully with those who sneered at the
    Dust Storms.
    Sweat days.
    Yellow people,
    Exiles.

---

[7] **pathos**—a mood of pity or sadness.

[8] **harbor**—to protect or conceal.

[9] **scoff**—to jeer or tease.

QUESTIONS TO CONSIDER

1. In "That Damned Fence," what does the fence symbolize?

2. What emotions about internment does "My Mom, Pop, and Me" evoke?

3. Do you agree that the Manzanar residents were probably "better, wiser" for their experience in the camp? Why or why not?

Life in the Camps

Barracks Newly built barracks made of flimsy material served as the homes for families.

Lined Up After long train and bus rides to the Relocation
Centers, Japanese Americans were assigned quarters in the barracks.
▼

▲

Horse Stalls These barracks for families
at the Tanforan Assembly Center in San Bruno,
California, are remodeled horse stalls.

Manzanar The dust swirling about the Relocation Center at Manzanar signaled the grim life the Japanese Americans had here.

▼

▲

Tule Lake A solitary man walks across the grounds at the Tule Lake
Relocation Center.

▲

Gardens People found ways to brighten even
these grim surroundings. Here a family has planted
a garden in front of their barracks at Tanforan
Assembly Center.

Pick-up Game Some Japanese boys play a game of pick-up basketball at a makeshift court at Tanforan. One of the barracks was set aside for games and recreation. These special "recreation" barracks were supervised by college-trained evacuee supervisors.

▼

Fighting in the Courts and on the Battlefields

"The Decision to End Detention"

In early 1943, with the war in the Pacific turning in favor of the American side, government officials began to look into ways to resettle the Japanese-American internees. They wanted to determine those who were loyal to the U.S. and give them work permits to allow them out of the camps. The WRA created a loyalty questionnaire which was given to every internee. The following is an excerpt from Personal Justice Denied, *the 1982 report of the Commission on Wartime Relocation and Internment of Civilians, describing the debates over detention and the loyalty questionnaire.*

By October 1942, the government held over 100,000 evacuees in relocation camps. After the tide of war turned with the American victory at Midway in June 1942, the possibility of serious Japanese attack was no longer **credible**;[1] detention and exclusion became increasingly difficult to defend. Nevertheless, other than an ineffective leave program run by the War Relocation

---

[1] **credible**—offering reasonable grounds for being believed.

Authority, the government had no plans to remedy the situation and no means of distinguishing the loyal from the disloyal. Total control of these civilians in the presumed interest of state security was rapidly becoming the accepted norm.

Determining the basis on which detention would be ended required the government to focus on the justification for controlling the ethnic Japanese. If the government took the position that race determined loyalty or that it was impossible to distinguish the loyal from the disloyal because "Japanese" patterns of thought and behavior were too alien to white Americans, there would be little incentive to end detention. If the government maintained the position that distinguishing the loyal from the disloyal was possible and that exclusion and detention were required only by the necessity of acting quickly under the threat of Japanese attack in early 1942, then a program to release those considered loyal should have been instituted in the spring of 1942 when people were confined in the assembly centers.

Neither position totally prevailed. General DeWitt and the Western Defense Command took the first position and opposed any review that would determine loyalty or threaten continued exclusion from the West Coast. Thus, there was no loyalty review during the assembly center period. Secretary Stimson and Assistant Secretary McCloy took the second view, but did not act on it until the end of 1942 and then only in a limited manner. At the end of 1942, over General DeWitt's opposition, Secretary Stimson, Assistant Secretary McCloy and General George C. Marshall, Chief of Staff, decided to establish a volunteer combat team of Nisei soldiers. The volunteers were to come from those who had passed a loyalty review. To avoid the obvious unfairness of allowing only those joining the military to establish their loyalty and leave the camps, the War Department joined WRA in expanding the loyalty review program to all adult evacuees.

This program was significant, but remained a compromise. It provided an opportunity to demonstrate loyalty to the United States on the battlefields; despite the human sacrifice involved, this was of immense practical importance in obtaining postwar acceptance for the ethnic Japanese. It opened the gates of the camps for some and began some reestablishment of normal life. But, with no apparent rationale or justification, it did not end exclusion of the loyal from the West Coast. The review program did not extend the presumption of loyalty to American citizens of Japanese descent, who were subject to an investigation and review not applied to other ethnic groups.

Equally important, although the loyalty review program was the first major government decision in which the interests of evacuees prevailed, the program was conducted so insensitively, with such lack of understanding of the evacuees' circumstances, that it became one of the most divisive and wrenching episodes of the camp detention.

After almost a year of what the evacuees considered utterly unjust treatment at the hands of the government, the loyalty review program began with filling out a questionnaire which posed two questions requiring declarations of complete loyalty to the United States. Thus, the questionnaire demanded a personal expression of position from each evacuee—a choice between faith in one's future in America and outrage at present injustice. Understandably most evacuees probably had deeply **ambiguous**[2] feelings about a government whose **rhetorical**[3] values of liberty and equality they wished to believe, but who found their present treatment in

---

[2] **ambiguous**—uncertain or doubtful.

[3] **rhetorical**—expressed in writing or speech.

painful contradiction to those values. The loyalty questionnaire left little room to express that ambiguity. Indeed, it provided an effective point of protest and organization against the government, from which more and more evacuees felt alienated. The questionnaire finally addressed the central question of loyalty that underlay the exclusion policy, a question which had been the predominant political and personal issue for the ethnic Japanese over the past year; answering it required confronting the conflicting emotions aroused by their relation to the government. Evacuee testimony shows the intensity of conflicting emotions:

> I answered both questions number 27 and 28 [the loyalty questions] in the negative, not because of disloyalty but due to the disgusting and shabby treatment given us. A few months after completing the questionnaire, U.S. Army officers appeared at our camp and gave us an interview to confirm our answers to the questions 27 and 28, and followed up with a question that in essence asked: "Are you going to give up or renounce your U.S. citizenship?" to which I promptly replied in the affirmative as a rebellious move. Sometime after the interview, a form letter from the Immigration and Naturalization Service arrived saying if I wanted to renounce my U.S. citizenship, sign the form letter and return. Well, I kept the Immigration and Naturalization Service waiting.

> Well, I am one of those that said "no, no" on it, one of the "no, no" boys, and it is not that I was proud about it, it was just that our legal rights were violated and I wanted to fight back. However, I didn't want to take this sitting down. I was really angry. It just got me so damned mad. Whatever we do, there was no

help from outside, and it seems to me that we are a race that doesn't count. So therefore, this was one of the reasons for the "no, no" answer.

Personal responses to the questionnaire inescapably became public acts open to community debate and scrutiny within the closed world of the camps. This made difficult choices **excruciating**:[4]

> After I volunteered for the [military] service, some people that I knew refused to speak to me. Some older people later questioned my father for letting me volunteer, but he told them that I was old enough to make up my own mind.

> The resulting infighting, beatings, and verbal abuses left families torn apart, parents against children, brothers against sisters, relatives against relatives, and friends against friends. So bitter was all this that even to this day, there are many amongst us who do not speak about that period for fear that the same harsh feelings might arise up again to the surface.

The loyalty review program was a point of decision and division for those in the camps. The avowedly loyal were eligible for release; those who were unwilling to profess loyalty or whom the government distrusted were segregated from the main body of evacuees into the Tule Lake camp, which rapidly became a center of disaffection and protest against the government and its policies—the unhappy refuge of evacuees consumed by anger and despair.

---

[4] **excruciating**—causing great pain or anguish.

QUESTIONS TO CONSIDER

1. What were the two government positions about what determined loyalty? That is, what was General DeWitt's position on loyalty versus that of Secretary Stimson and Assistant Secretary McCloy?

2. What in the end was the "loyalty review" and how was loyalty ultimately determined?

3. Who were the "no-no boys" and why were they pitted against others interned in the camps?

"Military Service"

Early in 1943, the U.S. government began to allow Japanese Americans to serve in the military. More than 33,000 Japanese Americans served their country during the war, and more than 18,000 of these had won release from internment camps by joining the military. It was an event of great irony: soldiers fighting and dying for a country that was holding their families behind barbed wire. Two units—the 100th Infantry Battalion and the 442nd Combat Team—of Japanese-American soldiers were created and both served with great distinction. In fact, the 442nd was the most decorated unit of the war. The following excerpt from Personal Justice Denied *is the Commission on Wartime Relocation and Internment of Civilians's summary of Japanese Americans' wartime service.*

In the spring of 1941, a few alert Army intelligence officers realized that, if war came, the Army would need Japanese language interpreters and translators. After much delay, Lieut. Col. John Weckerling and Capt. Kai Rasmussen won approval to start a small school for training persons with some background in Japanese. On November 1, 1941, the school opened at Crissy Field in San Francisco with four Nisei[1] instructors and 60 students, 58 of whom were Japanese Americans. The attack on Pearl Harbor confirmed the value of the program. During the spring of 1942, while evacuation was proceeding, the school was enlarged and transferred to Camp Savage in Minnesota. Meanwhile, the first group had completed training, and 35 of its graduates went to the Pacific—half to Guadalcanal and half to the Aleutian Islands.

The school, now renamed the Military Intelligence Service Language School (MISLS) and officially part of the War Department, began its first class at Camp Savage in June 1942 with 200 students. By the end of 1942, more than 100 Nisei had left for the Pacific. By Fall 1944, over 1,600 had graduated. When the school closed in 1946, after being moved once more to Fort Snelling, Minnesota, it had trained 6,000 men. Of these, 3,700 served in combat areas before the Japanese surrender. Ironically, the often-mistrusted Kibei—Japanese Americans who had received formal education in Japan—proved most qualified for the interpreter's task; most Nisei had too little facility with Japanese to be useful. As Mark Murakami pointed out:

> [On] the one hand the Japanese Americans were condemned for having the **linguistic**[2] and cultural knowledge of Japanese, and on the other hand the knowledge they had was **capitalized**[3] on and used as a secret weapon by the Army and Naval Intelligence.

At the beginning, MISLS graduates were poorly used in the Pacific. A few ended up fighting rather than using their rare language talent. Others were sent to

---

[1] Nisei—the first generation of ethnic Japanese born in the United States.

[2] **linguistic**—relating to language.

[3] **capitalized**—used to one's advantage.

remote, inactive outposts or were ineffectively employed by the Army. As the war went on, however, the situation improved as the Army learned how to use this valuable specialized resource.

Many of the linguists worked in teams, translating captured documents at intelligence centers around the Pacific. Large groups, for example, were posted in Australia, New Delhi and Hawaii. Their assignments included battle plans, defense maps, tactical orders, intercepted messages and diaries. From these, American commanders could anticipate enemy action, evaluate strengths and weaknesses, avoid surprise, and strike unexpectedly. The Nisei's first major accomplishment was translation of a document picked up on Guadalcanal; it completely listed Imperial Navy ships with their call signs and code names, and did the same for the Japanese Navy's air squadrons and bases. Among other accomplishments was translation of the entire Japanese naval battle plan for the Philippines as well as plans for defending the island.

In addition to rear-**echelon**[4] duties, language school graduates took part in combat, adding to their other duties interrogating enemy prisoners and persuading enemy soldiers to surrender. The first Nisei to help the Allies in actual combat through his language ability was Richard Sakakida, who translated a captured set of Japanese plans for a landing on Bataan early in the war; American tanks were able to move up and ambush the invaders as they arrived. One early group of linguists in a combat zone went to the Aleutian Islands. The linguists took part in every landing in the bitter island-hopping campaign through New Guinea, the Marianas, the Philippines and Okinawa, and participated in surrender ceremonies in Tokyo Bay. Nisei linguists served with about 130 different Army and Navy units, with the

---

[4] **echelon**—level of command; rank.

Marine Corps, and they were loaned to combat forces from Australia, New Zealand, England and China. Arthur Morimitsu's experiences make clear the range of demands on the linguists:

> This unit later joined other units to form the Mars Task Force, a commando unit. The mission was to cut off the enemy supply and reinforcements miles behind enemy lines along the Burma Road.
>
> We served as interpreters, questioned prisoners, translated the captured documents. We also worked as mule skinners, volunteered for patrol duty with advanced units and brought down dead and wounded soldiers from the battlefields.
>
> After we completed our duties with the Mars Task Force, I was sent back to New Delhi, India, assigned to the OSS, Office of Strategic Services, as head of a detachment of Nisei MIS to interrogate Japanese prisoners in preparation for the invasion of Japan.

After the surrender, MISLS shifted to civil matters, and its graduates helped to occupy and reconstruct Japan. They interpreted for military government teams, located and **repatriated**[5] imprisoned Americans, and interpreted at the war crimes trials. Despite their importance—General Willoughby, MacArthur's chief of intelligence, has said that the work of the Nisei MIS shortened the Pacific war by two years—these accomplishments got little publicity; most were classified information during the war. Instead, the highly-publicized exploits of the 100th Battalion and 442nd

---

[5] **repatriated**—restored or returned to one's own country.

Regimental Combat Team in Europe first helped to show where Nisei loyalty clearly lay.

THE 100TH BATTALION

The 100th Battalion began as part of the Hawaii National Guard. As evacuation plans were formulated on the mainland, the War Department also debated the best way to handle ethnic Japanese in Hawaii. On February 1, 1942, Hawaiian Commander Lieut. General Delos Emmons learned to his dismay that the War Department wanted to release the Nisei from active duty. He needed the manpower and had been impressed with the desire of many Hawaiian Nisei to prove their loyalty. After much discussion, Emmons recommended that a special Nisei Battalion be formed and removed to the mainland; General Marshall concurred. By June 5, 1942, 1,432 men—soon to be known as the 100th Battalion—had sailed. The battalion went to Camp McCoy, Wisconsin, for training and later to Camp Shelby in Mississippi. Over a year later, the group finally was ordered to North Africa, arriving on September 2, 1943.

From North Africa, the 100th immediately went north to Italy, promptly going into combat at Salerno on September 26. From then until March 1944, the 100th plunged into the bloody campaign which moved the Allies slowly up the Italian peninsula. The 100th suffered heavy casualties; 78 men were killed and 239 wounded or injured in the first month and a half alone. By the time the 100th finally pulled out, its effective strength was down to 521 men. The battalion had earned 900 Purple Hearts and the nickname "Purple Heart Battalion." As Warren Fencl, who fought near the 100th, said of it:

> The only time they ever had a desertion was from the hospital to get back to the front.

After a brief rest, the 100th was sent into the offensive from the Anzio beachhead, where it soon joined the other Nisei unit, the 442nd Regimental Combat Team.

THE 442ND REGIMENTAL COMBAT TEAM

While the 100th Battalion fought its way through Italy, the 442nd Regimental Combat Team had been formed and trained in Camp Shelby. Composed of volunteers from Hawaii and the mainland, many of whom came directly from relocation centers, the team trained from October 1943 to February 1944. Small groups left regularly to replace men from the 100th. On June 2, the 442nd landed at Naples and moved immediately to the beaches of Anzio. When the 442nd arrived, the 100th had already pushed toward Rome and engaged in heavy fighting. On June 15, the two came together and the 100th formally became part of the 442nd.

The 442nd fought through Belvedere, Luciana, and Livorno during the first half of the summer, finally pulling back for rest in late July. On July 27, Lieut. General Mark W. Clark, Commander of the Fifth Army, awarded the 100th a Presidential Unit Citation and commended the other units for their performance during the month, saying:

> You are always thinking of your country before yourselves. You have never complained through your long periods in the line. You have written a brilliant chapter in the history of the fighting men in America. You are always ready to close with the enemy, and you have always defeated him. The 34th Division is proud of you, the Fifth Army is proud of you, and the whole United States is proud of you.

On August 15, the 442nd went back into combat. Their first objective, to cross the Arno River, was accomplished early in September. Once again, the cost was great, for the unit's casualties totalled 1,272—more than one-fourth of its total strength.

From the Arno the 442nd moved to France to join the attack on the Vosges Mountains. Its first assignment was to take the town of Bruyeres, which was won after three days of bitter fighting. Describing the encounter, the Seventh Army reported:

> Bruyeres will long be remembered, for it was the most viciously fought-for town we had encountered in our long march against the Germans. The enemy defended it house by house, giving up a yard only when it became so **untenable**[6] they could no longer hope to hold it.

In the same month the 442nd encountered its bloodiest battle—rescue of the "Lost Battalion." Deep in the Vosges and meeting heavy German resistance, the 442nd was ordered to find and bring back a Texan battalion trapped nine miles away. For six days, the 442nd fought enemy infantry, artillery and tanks through forests and mountain ridges until it reached the Lost Battalion, suffering 800 casualties in a single week. They then pushed on for ten more days to take the ridge that was the Lost Battalion's original objective. From Bruyeres through the Vosges, the combat team had been cut to less than half its original strength. The casualty list numbered 2,000, of whom 140 had been killed. After another month of fighting, the 442nd finally came out of the line to rest. Sam Ozaki described arriving to join the 442nd after this engagement:

> The four others went overseas with the original 442nd. I joined them later as a replacement. I

---

[6] **untenable**—unreasonable; unjustified.

remember November 1944, when the replacements joined the 442nd, after they had pulled back from the Battle of Bruyeres, the lost battalion. I went looking for my buddies. I found one, Ted. Harry had been in a hospital, had been sent back to a hospital with a wound. The two others had been killed in action, saving the lost battalion.

After a relatively quiet winter of 1944–45 in the south of France, the 442nd moved back to Italy in March 1945. During its first assignment, to take a line of ridges, Pfc. Sadao Munemori took over his squad from a wounded leader. After destroying machine guns twenty feet ahead, he saw an enemy grenade fall into a nearby shell hole and dove on top of it, dying while saving his comrades. For this heroism Munemori received **posthumously**[7] the Congressional Medal of Honor. The 442nd now advanced into the rugged and heavily fortified Apennines. In a surprise attack following a secret all-night ascent through the mountains, the 442nd took their assigned peaks, thereby cracking the German defensive line. A diversionary move had turned into a full-scale offensive; from there, the unit continued northward until, on April 25, German resistance broke. By May 2, the war in Italy was over and, by May 9, the Germans had surrendered.

In seven major campaigns, the 442nd took 9,486 casualties—more than 300 percent of its original infantry strength, including 600 killed. More than 18,000 men served with the unit. Commenting on the painful loss of many fellow Nisei in the European theater, Masato Nakagawa admitted that "it was a high price to pay," but "[i]t was to prove our loyalty which was by no means an easy [task]." The 442nd was one of

---

[7] **posthumously**—occurring after one's death.

the war's most decorated combat teams, receiving seven Presidential Distinguished Unit Citations and earning 18,143 individual decorations—including one Congressional Medal of Honor, 47 Distinguished Service Crosses, 350 Silver Stars, 810 Bronze Stars and more than 3,600 Purple Hearts. As President Truman told members of the 442nd as he fastened the Presidential Unit banner to their regimental colors, these Nisei fought "not only the enemy, but prejudice."

OTHER NISEI SERVICE

Although the 442nd's **exploits**[8] are the most celebrated Nisei contribution to the war, many others played effective roles. FBI-trained Nisei operatives in the pre-war Philippines kept the Japanese population under surveillance. Others escaped the Army's segregation policy and served in other combat units. One Nisei even became an Air Force gunner and flew bombing missions over Tokyo. A small group served with Merrill's Marauders in Burma and a few were involved in the surrender of China.

Numerous others served in less glamorous but equally critical jobs. There were Nisei medics, mechanics and clerks in the Quartermaster Corps and Nisei women in the WACs. Nisei and Issei[9] served as language instructors, employees in the Army Map Service, and behind the scenes in the Office of Strategic Services (OSS) and Office of War Information (OWI). In the latter groups were primarily younger Issei who had fled Japan after World War I to avoid political persecution. At OWI and OSS, some made broadcasts to Japan, while others wrote propaganda leaflets urging Japanese troops to surrender or pamphlets dropped over Japan to weaken civilian morale.

---

[8] **exploits**—achievements; feats.

[9] Issei—the immigrant generation from Japan.

Although the exploits of the 442nd and 100th Battalion were publicized during the war, returning veterans still faced harassment and discrimination. Night riders warned Mary Masuda, whose brother had earned a posthumous Distinguished Service Cross, not to return to her home. A barber refused to give Captain Daniel Inouye a haircut. Mitsuo Usui's story is one that probably typifies the experiences of many returning veterans:

> Coming home, I was boarding a bus on Olympic Boulevard. A lady sitting in the front row of the bus, saw me and said, "Damn Jap." Here I was a proud American soldier, just coming back with my new uniform and new paratrooper boots, with all my campaign medals and awards, proudly displayed on my chest, and this? The bus driver upon hearing this remark, stopped the bus and said, "Lady, apologize to this American soldier or get off my bus"—She got off the bus.

> Embarrassed by the situation, I turned around to thank the bus driver. He said that's okay, buddy, everything is going to be okay from now on out. Encouraged by his comment, I thanked him and as I was turning away, I noticed a discharge pin on his lapel.

Men who had served with Nisei brought home stories of their heroism, and War Department officials praised the valuable service of the 442nd. The W R A sponsored speaking tours by returning veterans and officers who had served with them. On July 15, 1946, the men of the 442nd were received on the White House lawn by President Truman, who spoke eloquently of their bravery. In a few cases, military service led directly to community acceptance. In August 1946, *The Houston Press* ran a story about Sergeant George Otsuka, who had helped rescue the Lost Battalion, a Texas outfit, and was now being told to "keep away" from a farm he planned to purchase. Public response to the story was strong, and Sergeant Otsuka had no further trouble moving to his farm. Even on the West Coast, it was difficult to continue abusing veterans with an excellent record.

The Nisei had indeed distinguished themselves. As the **acerbic**[10] and distinguished General Joseph Stilwell said of Japanese Americans:

> They bought an awful hunk of America with their blood. . . . you're damn right those Nisei boys have a place in the American heart, now and forever. We cannot allow a single injustice to be done to the Nisei without defeating the purposes for which we fought.

---

[10] **acerbic**—sharp or biting in temper, mood, or tone.

QUESTIONS TO CONSIDER

1. Why is it ironic that the Kibei were often those most qualified for the task of interpreting?

2. How did the work of the Nisei MIS (Military Intelligence Service) help shorten the war?

3. What did President Truman mean when he said that the Nisei fought "not only the enemy, but prejudice"?

Nurse

BY MASAHARU HANE

Throughout the literature about the Japanese-American internment is the generally unstated conflict between Issei, Japanese immigrants to the United States, and the Nisei, the children of Issei, born and educated in the United States. Issei tended to be more tied to Japan than their children who knew only the American way of life. Masaharu Hane was an Issei interned at Poston during World War II. In the story "Nurse," an Issei observes and judges the behavior of a young Nisei woman. The story was first published in Poston Poetry, *the literary magazine of the camp.*

It was well past midnight when the Los Angeles-bound train from Denver pulled into Ashfork, Arizona. Sleepy-eyed soldiers with large duffel bags got off the train. This station is the transfer point for Wickenburg (Arizona). A few of us civilians followed them.

"Say, there's a Japanese!" exclaimed Mr. "O," my traveling companion, pointing in a general direction with his chin, since both his arms were loaded with suitcases. On looking, sure enough, there was a small Japanese girl standing behind a group of soldiers.

Around that time, it was quite a novelty to come across a Japanese while traveling by train, and we had longed to see even one. My eyes scanned the area in search of her parents or her brothers, but in vain.

An old conductor, **oblivious**[1] to the din being created by the soldiers, examined their tickets in minute detail, and herded them onto the coaches. I placed my hand baggage on the shelf, removed my coat, and gave a sigh of relief as I sat down.

As I mopped the perspiration from my brow, I looked around me. Then my gaze met that of the Japanese girl, who was seated across the aisle, and who I presume had been staring in this direction for quite some time. She was not as young as I had imagined the first time I saw her. All my doubts—as to her traveling alone in these times—were completely dispelled when I saw the Caucasian soldier seated next to her. That's it!—The girl was married to a white soldier, and she had come halfway to meet her husband, who was back on furlough!

Since they had come this far, it was a certainty that they were on their way to Poston, but my heart felt heavy, thinking of the feelings of this girl's parents.

As **cosmopolitan**[2] as I am, I do not yet quite relish the thought of marrying off my own daughter to either a Caucasian or a Negro. With my own conception, I imagined the embarrassment about to be caused her parents by her act of bringing this youth back to camp, and as I speculated on the pending heartache of her parents, I began to feel **morose**[3] and moody. The train started to move.

"Tickets, please—tickets." The old conductor checked the tickets again. He stuck a small check stub in the windows when he got through and went on to the next

---

[1] **oblivious**—unaware; lacking active conscious knowledge.

[2] **cosmopolitan**—worldly; sophisticated.

[3] **morose**—gloomy.

passenger. If the stubs were white, it meant that the passenger was getting off at the next transfer station; the red stubs were for through passengers.

After the conductor had gone by, I again looked at the young couple across the aisle. In this long travel by train, I have witnessed many "misbehaviors" on the part of the young people of this country. Naturally, these "misbehaviors" are thought to be so purely from my own point of view; from the standpoint of the people of this country, it could be their ordinary behavior. In any event, the sight of young girls and men seated near me, leaning on each other's shoulders, or using each other's lap for a pillow, disgusted me no end.

Oh well, no matter if Japanese blood coursed through this girl's veins; she was one that would marry a Caucasian. There is no reason to believe that her morality was not estranged from that of a true Japanese. Be that as it may, this girl consistently assumed a correct posture. The soldier, also, carried himself with **decorum**[4] and **deportment**.[5]

They were whispering to each other, but contrary to expectations, they did not enact a disgraceful scene.

Not only that, it did not appear that they were on too intimate terms. This caused me to throw overboard my original imagination regarding these two, and I determined anew that they were a brother and sister. I made up my mind that she was the young sister, and that she had an older brother who had features that resembled a Caucasian's. Unconsciously, I began to think that there was no mistaking his Caucasian features, but that somehow—it may have been just my fancy—he betrayed a mannerism characteristic of a Japanese.

At some unknown stop, the train picked up a few passengers, and we were on our way again. By this

---

[4] **decorum**—accepted standards of proper behavior.

[5] **deportment**—manner of conducting oneself.

time, there were no seats for the new passengers. One of them, a middle-aged man, stood in the aisle next to a seat where two middle-aged women were seated.

After examining the tickets of the new passengers, the conductor turned out the lights. Only one small globe was left burning, and the inside of the coach became dark.

It was about three o'clock in the morning. The soldiers were all fast asleep. I, too, being tired from the continuous train trip, began to feel drowsy. Suddenly, sensing a noise resembling someone's suppressed laughter, I awoke with a start. I looked in the direction whence the voice came.

The aforementioned middle-aged man, who was previously standing in the aisle, had just succeeded in squirming himself into the seat between the two middle-aged women. So revolting was the scene that I turned over, and started to close my eyes—but before I did so, I looked once more toward the Japanese girl.

The soldier brother appeared very tired as he slept, resting his head on his clenched fists, which were resting on the windowsill. The girl was seated erect, with her legs trimly together, but her right hand was placed over her forehead, obscuring her face.

I was unable to tell whether she was asleep or awake; [but assuming that she was asleep—trans.] in all my long experiences of train travel, I have never seen a man or woman who slept so correctly and properly as this girl.

Up until then, I felt ashamed, imagining that this girl had, contrary to the wishes of her parents, married a Caucasian, and that therefore, being such a girl, she would carry on in a disgraceful manner like the rest of the Caucasians; but now, on seeing the correct posture of this girl, I suddenly felt a sense of racial pride in being a member of the Japanese race. I smiled **sardonically**[6] at

---

[6] **sardonically**—scornfully; cynically.

my egotism, and to my own way of thinking to my own convenience.

However, I became distressed as I thought of the young girl with her odd "brother," and of their parents' feelings. Why did this girl try to avoid my glance? Could it be because she was ashamed of her brother? While thinking of such matters, I became drowsy again.

The aged conductor was shaking me by the arm. He informed me that we were due in Wickenburg in five minutes. Startled, I began to get ready to get off.

Dawn was completely upon us.

The Japanese girl was all prepared, and sitting formally erect. For the first time, I noticed that she was wearing a uniform. It was an extremely conservative neutral uniform in contrast to the W A C's.

I glanced at the check stub by the window. One was white—the other, red. The soldier was not getting off here with her.

Passing by the seat where the middle-aged man had squeezed his way between the two middle-aged women, and who was now sleeping with his arm embracing one of the women, I wound my way to the vestibule.

While waiting for the train to come to a complete stop, I asked this girl: "Where did you board this train?"

In clear-cut Japanese the girl answered: "I am on leave from the nurse's school in Colorado Springs."

QUESTIONS TO CONSIDER

1. When the narrator first sees the Japanese woman seated next to a white soldier, why does he feel "morose and moody"?

2. What behavior considered "normal" by American standards was repulsive to the narrator?

3. What's ironic about the young woman's response at the end?

Korematsu v. United States

OPINION OF THE U.S. SUPREME COURT

*Throughout the war, Japanese Americans fought the legality of their
internment. Three times cases came before the Supreme Court
arguing against Executive Order 9066 and the Wartime Relocation
Administration. In 1943, in the* Hirabayashi *case, the court unani-
mously upheld the right of the government to act because of
wartime conditions. In early 1944, in the* Korematsu *case, the court
stuck by its previous decision, but this time only by a vote of six to
three. Finally, in December 1944, the court ruled in the* Endo *case
that the U.S. government had no right to incarcerate law-abiding
citizens even in time of war. The camps began to close down
two weeks later. The following are excerpts from the opinions in
the* Korematsu *case, beginning with an excerpt from the majority
opinion and then excerpts from the* **dissenting**[1] *opinions of
Justices Murphy and Jackson.*

---

[1] **dissenting**—expressing a difference of opinion.

Mr. Justice Black Delivered the Opinion of the Court

It is said that we are dealing here with the case of imprisonment of a citizen in a concentration camp solely because of his ancestry, without evidence or inquiry concerning his loyalty and good disposition towards the United States. Our task would be simple, our duty clear, were this a case involving the imprisonment of a loyal citizen in a concentration camp because of racial prejudice. Regardless of the true nature of the assembly and relocation centers—and we deem it unjustifiable to call them concentration camps with all the ugly connotations that term implies—we are dealing specifically with nothing but an exclusion order. To cast this case into outlines of racial prejudice, without reference to the real military dangers which were presented, merely confuses the issue. Korematsu was not excluded from the Military Area because of hostility to him or his race. He was excluded because we are at war with the Japanese Empire, because the properly constituted military authorities feared an invasion of our West Coast and felt constrained to take proper security measures, because they decided that the military urgency of the situation demanded that all citizens of Japanese ancestry be segregated from the West Coast temporarily, and finally, because Congress, reposing its confidence in this time of war in our military leaders—as inevitably it must—determined that they should have the power to do just this. There was evidence of disloyalty on the part of some, the military authorities considered that the need for action was great, and time was short. We cannot—by availing ourselves of the calm perspective of hindsight—now say that at that time these actions were unjustified.

Affirmed.

Mr. Justice Murphy, Dissenting

This exclusion of "all persons of Japanese ancestry, both alien and non-alien," from the Pacific Coast area on a plea of military necessity in the absence of martial law[2] ought not to be approved. Such exclusion goes over "the very brink of constitutional power" and falls into the ugly **abyss**[3] of racism.

In dealing with matters relating to the prosecution and progress of a war, we must accord great respect and consideration to the judgments of the military authorities who are on the scene and who have full knowledge of the military facts. The scope of their **discretion**[4] must, as a matter of necessity and common sense, be wide. And their judgments ought not to be overruled lightly by those whose training and duties ill-equip them to deal intelligently with matters so vital to the physical security of the nation.

At the same time, however, it is essential that there be definite limits to military discretion, especially where martial law has not been declared. Individuals must not be left impoverished of their constitutional rights on a plea of military necessity that has neither substance nor support. Thus, like other claims conflicting with the asserted constitutional rights of the individual, the military claim must subject itself to the judicial process of having its reasonableness determined and its conflicts with other interests reconciled. "What are the allowable limits of military discretion, and whether or not they have been overstepped in a particular case, are judicial questions." . . .

It must be conceded that the military and naval situation in the spring of 1942 was such as to generate

---

[2] martial law—law by military force invoked by the government in times of crisis or emergency.

[3] **abyss**—a bottomless pit.

[4] **discretion**—the power to decide.

a very real fear of invasion of the Pacific Coast, accompanied by fears of sabotage and espionage in that area. The military command was therefore justified in adopting all reasonable means necessary to combat these dangers. In **adjudging**[5] the military action taken in light of the then apparent dangers, we must not erect too high or too meticulous standards; it is necessary only that the action have some reasonable relation to the removal of the dangers of invasion, sabotage and espionage. But the exclusion, either temporarily or permanently, of all persons with Japanese blood in their veins has no such reasonable relation. And that relation is lacking because the exclusion order necessarily must rely for its reasonableness upon the assumption that all persons of Japanese ancestry may have a dangerous tendency to commit sabotage and espionage and to aid our Japanese enemy in other ways. It is difficult to believe that reason, logic or experience could be marshalled in support of such an assumption.

That this forced exclusion was the result in good measure of this **erroneous**[6] assumption of racial guilt rather than bona fide military necessity is evidenced by the Commanding General's Final Report on the evacuation from the Pacific Coast area. In it he refers to all individuals of Japanese descent as "subversive," as belonging to "an enemy race" whose "racial strains are undiluted," and as constituting "over 112,000 potential enemies . . . at large today" along the Pacific Coast. In support of this blanket condemnation of all persons of Japanese descent, however, no reliable evidence is cited to show that such individuals were generally disloyal, or had generally so conducted themselves in this area as to constitute a special menace to defense installations or war industries, or had otherwise by their behavior

---

[5] **adjudging**—deciding by judicial opinion.

[6] **erroneous**—characterized by error; mistaken.

furnished reasonable ground for their exclusion as a group.

Justification for the exclusion is sought, instead, mainly upon questionable racial and sociological grounds not ordinarily within the realm of expert military judgment, supplemented by certain semi-military conclusions drawn from an unwarranted use of circumstantial evidence. Individuals of Japanese ancestry are condemned because they are said to be "a large, **unassimilated**,[7] tightly knit racial group, bound to an enemy nation by strong ties of race, culture, custom and religion." They are claimed to be given to "emperor worshipping ceremonies" and to "dual citizenship." Japanese language schools and allegedly pro-Japanese organizations are cited as evidence of possible group disloyalty, together with facts as to certain persons being educated and residing at length in Japan. It is intimated that many of these individuals deliberately resided "adjacent to strategic points," thus enabling them "to carry into execution a tremendous program of sabotage on a mass scale should any considerable number of them have been inclined to do so." The need for protective custody is also asserted. The report refers without identity to "numerous incidents of violence" as well as to other admittedly unverified or cumulative incidents. From this, plus certain other events not shown to have been connected with the Japanese Americans, it is concluded that the "situation was fraught with danger to the Japanese population itself" and that the general public "was ready to take matters into its own hands." Finally, it is intimated, though not directly charged or proved, that persons of Japanese ancestry were responsible for three minor isolated shellings and bombings of the Pacific Coast area, as well as for unidentified radio transmissions and night signalling.

---

[7] **unassimilated**—unable to adapt or conform to a different racial or cultural group.

The main reasons relied upon by those responsible for the forced evacuation, therefore, do not prove a reasonable relation between the group characteristics of Japanese Americans and the dangers of invasion, sabotage and espionage. The reasons appear, instead, to be largely an accumulation of much of the misinformation, half-truths and **insinuations**[8] that for years have been directed against Japanese Americans by people with racial and economic prejudices—the same people who have been among the foremost advocates of the evacuation. A military judgment based upon such racial and sociological considerations is not entitled to the great weight ordinarily given the judgments based upon strictly military considerations. Especially is this so when every charge relative to race, religion, culture, geographical location, and legal and economic status has been substantially discredited by independent studies made by experts in these matters.

The military necessity which is essential to the validity of the evacuation order thus resolves itself into a few **intimations**[9] that certain individuals actively aided the enemy, from which it is inferred that the entire group of Japanese Americans could not be trusted to be or remain loyal to the United States. No one denies, of course, that there were some disloyal persons of Japanese descent on the Pacific Coast who did all in their power to aid their ancestral land. Similar disloyal activities have been engaged in by many persons of German, Italian and even more pioneer stock in our country. But to infer that examples of individual disloyalty prove group disloyalty and justify discriminatory action against the entire group is to deny that under our system of law individual guilt is the sole basis for deprivation of rights. Moreover, this inference, which is at the

---

[8] **insinuations**—acts that introduce an idea subtly or indirectly.

[9] **intimations**—hinted suggestions.

very heart of the evacuation orders, has been used in support of the abhorrent and despicable treatment of minority groups by the dictatorial tyrannies which this nation is now pledged to destroy. To give constitutional sanction to that inference in this case, however well-intentioned may have been the military command on the Pacific Coast, is to adopt one of the cruelest of the rationales used by our enemies to destroy the dignity of the individual and to encourage and open the door to discriminatory actions against other minority groups in the passions of tomorrow. . . .

I dissent, therefore, from this legalization of racism. Racial discrimination in any form and in any degree has no justifiable part whatever in our democratic way of life. It is unattractive in any setting but it is utterly revolting among a free people who have embraced the principles set forth in the Constitution of the United States. All residents of this nation are kin in some way by blood or culture to a foreign land. Yet they are primarily and necessarily a part of the new and distinct civilization of the United States. They must accordingly be treated at all times as the heirs of the American experiment and as entitled to all the rights and freedoms guaranteed by the Constitution.

Mr. Justice Jackson, Dissenting

Korematsu was born on our soil, of parents born in Japan. The Constitution makes him a citizen of the United States by **nativity**[10] and a citizen of California by residence. No claim is made that he is not loyal to this country. There is no suggestion that apart from the matter involved here he is not law-abiding and well disposed. Korematsu, however, has been convicted of an act not commonly a crime. It consists merely of being

---

[10] **nativity**—birth.

present in the state whereof he is a citizen, near the place where he was born, and where all his life he has lived.

Even more unusual is the series of military orders which made this conduct a crime. They forbid such a one to remain, and they also forbid him to leave. They were so drawn that the only way Korematsu could avoid violation was to give himself up to the military authority. This meant submission to custody, examination, and transportation out of the territory, to be followed by immediate confinement in detention camps.

A citizen's presence in the locality, however, was made a crime only if his parents were of Japanese birth. Had Korematsu been one of four—the others being, say, a German alien enemy, an Italian alien enemy, and a citizen of American-born ancestors, convicted of treason but out on parole—only Korematsu's presence would have violated the order. The difference between their innocence and his crime would result, not from anything he did, said, or thought, different than they, but only in that he was born of different racial stock.

Now, if any fundamental assumption underlies our system, it is that guilt is personal and not inheritable. Even if all of one's antecedents had been convicted of treason, the Constitution forbids its penalties to be visited upon him, for it provides that "no attainder of treason shall work corruption of blood, or forfeiture except during the life of the person attainted." But here is an attempt to make an otherwise innocent act a crime merely because this prisoner is the son of parents as to whom he had no choice, and belongs to a race from which there is no way to resign. If Congress in peacetime legislation should enact such a criminal law, I should suppose this Court would refuse to enforce it.

QUESTIONS TO CONSIDER

1. On what grounds did the opinion of the court (delivered by Justice Black) uphold the exclusion order?

2. On what grounds did Justice Murphy dissent?

3. On what grounds did Justice Jackson dissent?

4. Given the evidence from both sides, do you think the Supreme Court decision was fair? Why or why not?

chapter four

Remembrance
and Redress

Poetry: The Next Generation

After the internment ended, Japanese Americans picked up the threads of their lives as best they could. Few spoke about the internment or the war. The next generation of Japanese Americans, those who had no direct experience of the camps, began in the 1970s to show great interest in what had happened. They took it upon themselves to break the silence of their parents and grandparents. Poets and novelists have led the way in examining what happened to Japanese Americans during the war, lending a voice where little was heard before. The poets Janice Mirikitani and Richard Oyama have both written about the phenomenon of silence and putting memories down on paper.

Breaking Silence

BY JANICE MIRIKITANI

For my mother's testimony before Commission on Wartime Relocation and Internment of Japanese-American Civilians

There are miracles that happen
she said.
From silences
in the glass caves of our ears,
from the crippled tongue,
from the mute, wet eyelash,
testimonies waiting like winter.
   we were told
that silence was better
golden like our skin,
   useful like
go quietly,
   easier like
don't make waves,
   expedient[1] like
horsetails and deserts.

    "Mr. Commissioner . . .
    U.S. Army Signal Corps confiscated
    our property . . . it was subjected to vandalism
    and **ravage.**[2] All improvements we had made
    before our incarceration was stolen
    or destroyed . . .
    I was **coerced**[3] into signing documents
    giving you authority to take . . . "
    . . . to take
    . . . to take.

My mother,
soft like **tallow,**[4]
words peeling from her
like slivers
of yellow flame,

---

[1] **expedient**—serving to promote a desired end; convenient.

[2] **ravage**—to lay waste; devastate.

[3] **coerced**—forced.

[4] **tallow**—a substance used for making candles and soap.

her testimony
a vat of boiling water
surging through the coldest
bluest vein.
   She, when the land labored
with flowers, their scent
flowing into her pores,
had molded her earth
like a woman
with soft breasted slopes
yielding silent mornings
and purple noisy birthings,
yellow hay
and tomatoes throbbing
like the sea.
   And then
all was hushed for announcements:
   "Take only what you can carry . . ."
We were made to believe
our faces betrayed us.
Our bodies were loud
with yellow
screaming flesh
needing to be silenced
behind barbed wire.

       "Mr. Commissioner . . .
        . . . it seems we were singled out
       from others who were under suspicion.
       Our neighbors were of German and Italian
       descent, some of whom were not citizens . . .
       It seems we were singled out . . . "

She had worn her sweat
like lemon leaves
shining on the rough edges of work,
removed the mirrors

from her rooms
so she would not be tempted
by vanity.
    Her dreams
honed[5] the blade of her plow.
The land,
the building of food was
noisy as the opening of irises.
The sounds of work
bolted in barracks . . .
silenced.

    Mr. Commissioner . . .
    So when you tell me I must limit testimony
    to 5 minutes, when you tell me my time is up,
    I tell you this:
    Pride has kept my lips
    pinned by nails
    my rage coffined.
    But I **exhume**[6] my past
    to claim this time.
    My youth is buried in Rohwer,
    Obachan's ghost visits Amache Gate,
    My niece haunts Tule Lake.
    Words are better than tears,
    so I spill them.
        I kill this, the silence . . .

There are miracles that happen,
she said,
and everything is made visible.
    We see the cracks and fissures in our soil:
We speak of suicides and intimacies,
of longings lush like wet **furrows**,[7]

---

[5] **honed**—sharpened.

[6] **exhume**—dig up something buried (especially a body).

[7] **furrows**—trenches in the earth, as made by a plow.

of oceans bearing us toward imagined riches,
of burning humiliations and
crimes by the government.
Of self hate and of love that breaks
through silences.
    We are lightning and justice.
    Our souls become transparent like glass
revealing tears for war-dead sons
red ashes of Hiroshima
jagged wounds from barbed wire.
    We must recognize ourselves at last
    We are a rain forest of color
and noise.
    We hear everything.
    We are unafraid.

            Our language is beautiful.

    *(Quoted excerpts from my mother's testimony modified
with her permission— J.M.)*

In Remembrance

BY JANICE MIRIKITANI

We gather at your coffin,
Uncle Minoru.
Mother, with her hands like gardenias,
touches your sleeves.
We whisper of how well you look
peaceful in your utter silence.
How much we remember.
Why so much now, at death?
    Your kindnesses, Uncle,

as you crafted paper monkeys,
multicolored birds
to climb and jerk on a stick
to amuse children who gathered
at your innocent dark eyes,
always slightly moist.
We would jump on your back, riding you
like a silent horse,
as you lumbered on your hands and knees
from room to room.
     How much we remember . . .
We rode your shoulders,
knotted with hurt,
dressed in faded denim, smelling like
laundry soap and fish.
You never complained of it
only through those dark moist eyes,
and your smile that drew
living animals to you, even wild birds.
Obachan said they could smell
the wounds hiding in your throat,
the wound in your heart
pierced by unjust punishment, racism, and rejection
sharp as blades.
     When did you vow silence, Minoru?
After the camps,
after you buried a daughter?
You slumped into a light
of your own and let life ride you.
Your daughter thrown broken
on the road by a drunk driver
who mumbled she flew from nowhere like a dumb chicken,
stretched out $200, not one apology,
and said we were safer in the camps.
     Was there nothing left to say, Minoru,
as you slapped away his hot white hand?

How much we remember . . .
When they took you to Amache Gate
locked us up like herded horses,
your dark innocent eyes, moist
with disbelief at charges of
sabotage, espionage,
your shoulders staggered from the lies.
Fear like a cold finger
pressed at your heart.
The sky scummed over with clouds
and punishment without crime
stabbed between the blades of your back.
    Was there nothing left to say?
Minoru, the children who rode you
have tongues like birds.
We chatter. We remember
the mounds of hurt at your shoulders.
Could we but massage them to soothe
the pain, but death
makes our regrets scattered as apologies.
We did not expect them
to rip the coat of pride from your bones
nor the melody from your throat.
    Yes, there is much to say.
We will not leave your memory
as a silent **rancid**[8] rose.
Our tongues become **livid**[9] with history and
demands for reparations.
Crimes are revealed like the bloody lashes
of a fallen whip:
    the falsehoods, deletions, the conspiracy
    to legalize mass imprisonment.
No, we will not forget

---

[8] **rancid**—having a tainted smell or taste.
[9] **livid**—furiously angry.

Amache Gate, Rohwer, Poston, Heart Mountain,
Minidoka, Jerome, Gila River, Manzanar,
Topaz, Tule Lake.
Our tongues are sharp like blades.
We overturn furrows of secrecy.
   Yes, we will harvest justice.
And Uncle, perhaps
your spirit will return
alive in a horse, or a bird,
riding free in the wind
life surging through
the **sinews**[10] of your strong shoulders.
   And yes,
the struggle continues on
with our stampede of voices.

When We Were Children

BY RICHARD OYAMA

When we were children,
you spoke Japanese
in lowered voices
between yourselves.

Once you uttered secrets
which we should not know,
were not to be heard by us.
When you spoke
of some dark secret
you would **admonish**[11] us,
"Don't tell it to anyone else."
It was a suffocated vow of silence.

---

[10] **sinews**—tendons.
[11] **admonish**—to warn against something.

What we have come to know
Yet cannot tell
lingers like voiceless ghosts
wandering in our memory
as though memory is
desert bleached by
years of cruel exile.

It is the language
of silence within myself
I cannot fill with words
the sound of **mournful**[12] music
distantly heard.

---

[12] **mournful**—sad; sorrowful.

QUESTIONS TO CONSIDER

1. According to the speaker in "Breaking Silence," what are the harmful effects of remaining silent?

2. How does the speaker in "In Remembrance" plan to "harvest justice"?

3. What reason for his parents' silence does Richard Oyama offer in his poem?

from

Farewell to Manzanar

BY JEANNE WAKATSUKI HOUSTON AND JAMES D. HOUSTON

Jeanne Wakatsuki was seven years old when her family was interned at Manzanar camp. Her book Farewell to Manzanar *recreates what life was like in Manzanar and how she came to terms with the experience. Thirty years after her internment, Wakatsuki returned to Manzanar with her husband and her three children. The following excerpt from* Farewell to Manzanar *describes that return journey.*

It was April 1972, thirty years almost to the day, that we piled our three kids into the car and headed out there. From where we live now, in the California coast town of Santa Cruz, it's a full day's drive. We started down 101 to Paso Robles, crossed over the hummocky Diablo Range to the central valley, skirted Bakersfield, and climbed through Tehachapi Pass into the desert.

At Mojave we turned north onto the same road our bus had taken out from Los Angeles in April 1942. It is the back road to the Sierras and the main route from southern California to Reno and Lake Tahoe. We joined bikers and backpackers and the skiers heading for Mammoth. The traffic through there is fast, everyone but the bikers making for the high country. As we sped along wide roads at sixty and seventy, with our kids exclaiming at the sights we passed and our car loaded down with camping gear, it seemed even more incredible to me that a place like Manzanar could have been anywhere within reach of such a highway, such a caravan of pleasure-seeking travelers.

The bikers peeled off at Red Rock Canyon, a gorgeous bulge of pink cliffs and rusty gulches humping out of the flatlands. After that it was lovely desert but nothing much to stop for. In a hundred miles we passed two **oases**,[1] the first at Olancha, the second around Lone Pine, a small, tree-filled town where a lot of mountain buffs turn off for the Mount Whitney Portal.

A few miles out of Lone Pine we started looking for another stand of trees, some tall elms, and what remains of those **gnarled**[2] pear orchards. They were easy to spot. Everything else is sagebrush, tumbleweeds, and wind.

At its peak, in the summer of '42, Manzanar was the biggest city between Reno and Los Angeles, a special kind of western boom town that sprang from the sand, flourished, had its day, and now has all but disappeared. The barracks are gone, torn down right after the war. The guard towers are gone, and the mess halls and shower rooms, the hospital, the tea gardens, and the white buildings outside the compound. Even the dust is gone. Spreading brush holds it to the ground. Thirty

---

[1] **oases**—fertile or green areas in an otherwise arid region.

[2] **gnarled**—knotty; twisted.

years earlier, army bulldozers had scraped everything clean to start construction.

What you see from the road are the two gatehouses, each a small empty pillbox of a building faced with flagstones and topped, like tiny **pagodas,**[3] with shingled curving roofs. Farther in, you see the elms, most of which were planted by internees, and off to the right a large green building that was once our high school auditorium, now a maintenance depot for the Los Angeles Power and Water District, who leased the land to the government during the war and still owns it.

Past the gatehouses we turned left over a cattle guard and onto a dirt perimeter road that led to the far side of the campsite. About half a mile in we spotted a white **obelisk**[4] gleaming in the distance and marking a subtle line where the plain begins gradually to slope upward into the alluvial fan[5] that becomes the base of the mountains. It seemed miraculous, as if some block of stone had fallen from the peaks above and landed upright in the brush, chiseled, solitary, twelve feet high.

Near it a dozen graves were outlined in the sand with small stones, and a barbed-wire fence surrounded them to keep back the cattle and the tumbleweed. The black Japanese script cut into the white face of the obelisk read simply, "A Memorial to the Dead."

We were alone out there, too far from the road to hear anything but wind. I thought of Mama, now seven years gone. For a long time I stood gazing at the monument. I couldn't step inside the fence. I believe in ghosts and spirits. I knew I was in the presence of those who had died at Manzanar. I also felt the spiritual presence that always lingers near awesome wonders like Mount Whitney. Then, as if rising from the ground around us

---

[3] **pagodas**—Far Eastern towers, usually erected as temples.

[4] **obelisk**—an upright pillar that tapers gradually as it rises, ending in a pyramid.

[5] alluvial fan—junction where a tributary or small stream meets a main stream.

on the valley floor, I began to hear the first whispers, nearly inaudible, from all those thousands who once had lived out here, a wide, windy sound of the ghost of that life. As we began to walk, it grew to a murmur, a thin steady hum.

We turned the kids loose, watched them scamper off ahead of us, and we followed what used to be an asphalt road running from the back side of the camp a mile out to the highway. The obelisk—built in 1943—and the gatehouses are all that have survived intact from internment days. The rest of the place looks devastated by a bombing raid.

The old road was disintegrating, split, weed-sprung. We poked through the remains of hospital foundations, undermined by erosion channels. We found concrete slabs where the latrines and shower rooms stood, and irrigation ditches, and here and there, the small rock arrangements that once decorated many of the entranceways. I had found out that even in North Dakota, when Papa and the other Issei men imprisoned there had free time, they would gather small stones from the plain and spend hours sorting through a dry stream bed looking for the veined or polished rock that somehow pleased the most. It is so characteristically Japanese, the way lives were made more tolerable by gathering loose desert stones and forming with them something enduringly human. These rock gardens had outlived the barracks and the towers and would surely outlive the asphalt road and rusted pipes and shattered slabs of concrete. Each stone was a mouth, speaking for a family, for some man who had beautified his doorstep.

Vegetation gets thickest toward the center of the site, where the judo pavilion once stood and where rows of elms planted as windbreaks have tripled their growth since the forties. In there we came across the remains of a small park. A stone-lined path ran along the base of a broad mound of dirt about five feet high. Stones had been arranged on the mound, and some low trees still shaded it and made an arch above the path. For a moment I was strolling again, finding childish comfort in its **incongruous**[6] design.

But after ten feet the path ended in tumbleweeds. The trees were dry and stubby, the mound was barren, and my attention was arrested by a water faucet sticking two feet out of the sand, like some subterranean periscope. One of these had provided water for each barracks. They stuck up at intervals in every direction, strangely sharpening the loneliness and desolation, sometimes the only sign of human presence in an acre or two of sand.

My mood had shifted. The murmur turned to wind. For a while I could almost detach myself from the place and its history and take pleasure in it purely as an archeological site. I saw the outlines, patterns this city must have taken. I imagined where the buildings stood, almost as I once did nosing around old Roman villas in Europe. We saw a low ring of stones built up with cement and wondered who the mason was who knelt there and studied the shapes before fitting them together. We moved around the ring a few feet to find out. This was the old flagpole circle, where the Stars and Stripes were hoisted every morning, and the inscription scratched across the top said, BUILT BY WADA AND CREW, JUNE 10, 1942 A.D.

The A.D. made me shiver. I knew that the man who inscribed it had foreseen these ruins and did not want his masonry identified with the wrong era. His words coming out of the stone became a voice that merged with all the others, not a murmur this time, but low voices muttering and chattering all around me. We were crossing what used to be a firebreak, now a sandy field devoid of any growth. The wind was vicious there,

---

[6] **incongruous**—not harmonious; internally inconsistent.

with nothing to break it, and the voices grew. The fire-break was where we had talent shows and dances and outdoor movies in the summer, and where the kids played games. I heard the girls' glee club I used to sing in, way off from the other side of camp, their tiny grade-school sopranos singing, "Beautiful dreamer, wake unto me." I closed my eyes and I was ten years old again. Nothing had changed. I heard laughter. It was almost dusk, the wind had dropped, and I saw old men squatting in the dirt, Papa and some of his cronies, muttering and smoking their cigarettes. In the summertime they used to burn orange peels under gallon cans, with holes punched in the sides, to keep the mosquitoes away. Sometimes they would bring out their boards to play *goh* and *hana*. The orange peels would smolder in there, and the men would hunker down around the cans and watch the smoke seep out the holes.

From that firebreak we cut across toward the first row of pear trees, looking for what might remain of Block 28. There wasn't much to guide us but the trees themselves and a view I remembered of the blunt, bulky Inyo Range that bounds the eastern limit of the valley. When we were close enough to smell the trees we stopped. They were stunted, **tenacious**,[7] tough the way a cactus has to be. The water table in that one area has kept them living through all these years of neglect, and they were ready to bloom at any moment. The heady smell was as odd in that desert setting as the little scrap of park had been, as odd yet just as familiar. We used to picnic there in blossom time, on weekends, if we got a wind-free day.

The wind blew it toward us now—chilled pear nectar—and it blew our kids around a high stand of brush. They came tumbling across the sand, demanding to know what we were going to do out here. Our twins

---

[7] **tenacious**—tough, not easily pulled apart.

were five years old at the time, a boy and a girl. Our older daughter had just turned eleven. She knew about "the evacuation," but it would be a few more years before she absorbed this part of the family history. For these three the site had been like any wreck or ruin. They became explorers, rushed around hoping the next clump of dusty trees or chunk of wall might reveal the treasure, the trinket, the exotically rusted hinge. Nothing much had turned up. The shine was wearing off the trip. Their eyes were red and their faces badly chapped. No place for kids.

My husband started walking them back to the car. I stayed behind a moment longer, first watching our eleven-year-old stride ahead, leading her brother and sister. She has long dark hair like mine and was then the same age I had been when the camp closed. It was so simple, watching her, to see why everything that had happened to me since we left camp referred back to it, in one way or another. At that age your body is changing, your imagination is galloping, your mind is in that zone between a child's vision and an adult's. Papa's life ended at Manzanar, though he lived for twelve more years after getting out. Until this trip I had not been able to admit that my own life really began there. The times I thought I had dreamed it were one way of getting rid of it, part of wanting to lose it, part of what you might call a whole Manzanar mentality I had lived with for twenty-five years. Much more than a remembered place, it had become a state of mind. Now, having seen it, I no longer wanted to lose it or to have those years erased. Having found it, I could say what you can only say when you've truly come to know a place: Farewell.

I had nearly outgrown the shame and the guilt and the sense of unworthiness. This visit, this **pilgrimage**,[8] made comprehensible, finally, the traces that remained

---

[8] **pilgrimage**—a journey of a pilgrim, usually to a shrine or sacred place.

and would always remain, like a needle. That hollow ache I carried during the early months of internment had shrunk, over the years, to a tiny sliver of suspicion about the very person I was. It had grown so small sometimes I'd forget it was there. Months might pass before something would remind me. When I first read, in the summer of 1972, about the pressure Japan's economy was putting on American business and how a union in New York City had printed up posters of an American flag with MADE IN JAPAN written across it, then that needle began to jab. I heard Mama's soft, weary voice from 1945 say, "It's all starting over." I knew it wouldn't. Yet neither would I have been surprised to find the FBI at my door again. I would resist it much more than my parents did, but deep within me something had been prepared for that. Manzanar would always live in my nervous system, a needle with Mama's voice.

QUESTIONS TO CONSIDER

1. How were the people interned at Manzanar like the tenacious pear trees (paragraph 16) that still grow there?

2. What does the writer's pilgrimage to Manzanar mean to her?

3. Do you think internment like that which occurred during World War II could ever take place again in this country? Explain why or why not.

An American Promise

BY PRESIDENT GERALD FORD

The year 1976 was the bicentennial of the United States. On February 20, 1976, President Gerald Ford signed a proclamation that was an apology to the Japanese Americans who were interned during World War II. It was appropriate that in a year of celebration of the country and its ideals, Americans also owned up to the darker aspects of the country's history.

A Proclamation

In this Bicentennial Year, we are commemorating the anniversary dates of many of the great events in American history. An honest reckoning, however, must include a recognition of our national mistakes as well as our national achievements. Learning from our mistakes is not pleasant, but as a great philosopher once admonished, we must do so if we want to avoid repeating them.

February 19th is the anniversary of a sad day in American history. It was on that date in 1942, in the midst of the response to the hostilities that began on December 7, 1941, that Executive Order No. 9066 was issued, subsequently enforced by the criminal penalties of a statute enacted March 21, 1942, resulting in the uprooting of loyal Americans. Over one hundred thousand persons of Japanese ancestry were removed from their homes, detained in special camps, and eventually relocated.

The tremendous effort by the War Relocation Authority and concerned Americans for the welfare of these Japanese Americans may add perspective to that story, but it does not erase the setback to fundamental American principles. Fortunately, the Japanese-American community in Hawaii was spared the indignities suffered by those on our mainland.

We now know what we should have known then—not only was that evacuation wrong, but Japanese Americans were and are loyal Americans. On the battlefield and at home, Japanese Americans—names like Hamada, Mitsumori, Marimoto, Noguchi, Yamasaki, Kido, Munemori and Miyamura—have been and continue to be written in our history for the sacrifices and the contributions they have made to the well-being and security of this, our common Nation.

The Executive order that was issued on February 19, 1942, was for the sole purpose of prosecuting the war with the Axis Powers, and ceased to be effective with the end of those hostilities. Because there was no formal statement of its termination, however, there is concern among many Japanese Americans that there may yet be some life in that **obsolete**[1] document. I think it appropriate, in this our Bicentennial Year, to remove all

---

[1] **obsolete**—no longer in use; outmoded.

doubt on that matter, and to make clear our commitment in the future.

NOW, THEREFORE, I, GERALD R. FORD, President of the United States of America, do hereby proclaim that all the authority **conferred**[2] by Executive Order No. 9066 terminated upon the issuance of Proclamation No. 2714, which formally proclaimed the **cessation**[3] of the hostilities of World War II on December 31, 1946.

I call upon the American people to affirm with me this American Promise—that we have learned from the tragedy of that long-ago experience forever to treasure liberty and justice for each individual American, and resolve that this kind of action shall never again be repeated.

IN WITNESS WHEREOF, I have hereunto set my hand this nineteenth day of February in the year of our Lord nineteen hundred seventy-six, and of the Independence of the United States of America the two hundredth.

GERALD R. FORD

---

[2] **conferred**—given, betowed.

[3] **cessation**—a final stopping of an action.

QUESTIONS TO CONSIDER

1. How does Ford put to rest the fears that Japanese Americans could be relocated again?

2. What is the "promise" Ford asked all American people to make?

"Summary"

The Commission on Wartime Relocation and Internment of Civilians (CWRIC) explicitly compared the treatment of Japanese Americans to that of German Americans and Italian Americans with disturbing conclusions. The following section from the CWRIC's 1982 report Personal Justice Denied *explores those comparisons and ends with the Committee's recommendations to Congress in 1983.*

The Comparisons

To either side of the Commission's account of the exclusion, removal and detention, there is a version argued by various witnesses that makes a radically different analysis of the events. Some contend that, forty years later, we cannot recreate the atmosphere and events of 1942 and that the extreme measures taken then were solely to protect the nation's safety when there was no reasonable alternative. Others see in these events only the **animus**[1] of racial hatred directed toward people whose skin was not white. Events in Hawaii in World War II and

---

[1] **animus**—bad intention; ill will.

the historical treatment of Germans and German Americans shows that neither analysis is satisfactory.

Hawaii. When Japan attacked Pearl Harbor, nearly 158,000 persons of Japanese ancestry lived in Hawaii—more than 35 percent of the population. Surely, if there were dangers from espionage, sabotage and fifth column activity by American citizens and resident aliens of Japanese ancestry, danger would be greatest in Hawaii, and one would anticipate that the most swift and severe measures would be taken there. But nothing of the sort happened. Less than 2,000 ethnic Japanese in Hawaii were taken into custody during the war—barely one percent of the population of Japanese descent. Many factors contributed to this reaction.

Hawaii was more ethnically mixed and racially tolerant than the West Coast. Race relations in Hawaii before the war were not infected with the same virulent antagonism of 75 years of agitation. While anti-Asian feeling existed in the territory, it did not represent the longtime views of well-organized groups as it did on the West Coast and, without statehood, **xenophobia**[2] had no effective voice in the Congress.

The larger population of ethnic Japanese in Hawaii was also a factor. It is one thing to vent frustration and historical prejudice on a scant two percent of the population; it is very different to disrupt a local economy and tear a social fabric by locking up more than one-third of a territory's people. And in Hawaii the half-measure of exclusion from military areas would have been meaningless.

In large social terms, the Army had much greater control of day-to-day events in Hawaii. Martial law was declared in December 1941, suspending the writ of

---

[2] **xenophobia**—fear or hatred of anything or anyone foreign.

habeas corpus, so that through the critical first months of the war, the military's recognized power to deal with any emergency was far greater than on the West Coast.

Individuals were also significant in the Hawaiian equation. The War Department gave great discretion to the commanding general of each defense area and this brought to bear very different attitudes toward persons of Japanese ancestry in Hawaii and on the West Coast. The commanding general in Hawaii, Delos Emmons, restrained plans to take radical measures, raising practical problems of labor shortages and transportation until the pressure to evacuate the Hawaiian Islands subsided. General Emmons does not appear to have been a man of **dogmatic**[3] racial views; he appears to have argued quietly but consistently for treating the ethnic Japanese as loyal to the United States, absent evidence to the contrary.

This policy was clearly much more congruent with basic American law and values. It was also a much sounder policy in practice. The remarkably high rate of enlistment in the Army in Hawaii is in sharp contrast to the doubt and alienation that marred the recruitment of Army volunteers in the relocation camps. The wartime experience in Hawaii left behind neither the extensive economic losses and injury suffered on the mainland nor the psychological burden of the direct experience of unjust exclusion and detention.

The German Americans. The German-American experience in the First World War was far less traumatic and damaging than that of the ethnic Japanese in the Second World War, but it underscores the power of war fears and war hysteria to produce irrational but emotionally powerful reactions to people whose ethnicity links them to the enemy.

---

[3] **dogmatic**—having to do with views that are strongly held but not adequately supported.

There were obvious differences between the position of people of German descent in the United States in 1917 and the ethnic Japanese at the start of the Second World War. In 1917, more than 8,000,000 people in the United States had been born in Germany or had one or both parents born there. Although German Americans were not massively represented politically, their numbers gave them notable political strength and support from political spokesmen outside the ethnic group.

The history of the First World War bears a suggestive resemblance to the events of 1942: rumors in the press of sabotage and espionage, use of a stereotype of the German as an unassimilable and **rapacious**[4] Hun, followed by an effort to suppress those institutions—the language, the press and the churches—that were most palpably foreign and perceived as the seedbed of Kaiserism. There were numerous examples of official and quasi-governmental harassment and fruitless investigation of German Americans and resident German aliens. This history is made even more disturbing by the absence of an extensive history of anti-German agitation before the war.

The **promulgation**[5] of Executive Order 9066 was not justified by military necessity, and the decisions which followed from it—detention, ending detention and ending exclusion—were not driven by analysis of military conditions. The broad historical causes which shaped these decisions were race prejudice, war hysteria and a failure of political leadership. Widespread ignorance of Japanese Americans contributed to a policy conceived in haste and executed in an atmosphere of fear and anger at Japan. A grave injustice was done to American citizens and resident aliens of Japanese ancestry who, without individual review or any probative evidence

---

[4] **rapacious**—preying on others; craving power or another's possessions.

[5] **promulgation**—the act of putting a law into effect.

against them, were excluded, removed and detained by the United States during World War II.

In memoirs and other statements after the war, many of those involved in the exclusion, removal and detention passed judgment on those events. While believing in the context of the time that evacuation was a legitimate exercise of the war powers, Henry L. Stimson recognized that "to loyal citizens this forced evacuation was a personal injustice." In his autobiography, Francis Biddle reiterated his beliefs at the time: "the program was ill-advised, unnecessary and unnecessarily cruel." Justice William O. Douglas, who joined the majority opinion in *Korematsu* which held the evacuation constitutionally permissible, found that the evacuation case "was ever on my conscience." Milton Eisenhower described the evacuation to the relocation camps as "an inhuman mistake." Chief Justice Earl Warren, who had urged evacuation as Attorney General of California, stated, "I have since deeply regretted the removal order and my own testimony advocating it, because it was not in keeping with our American concept of freedom and the rights of citizens." Justice Tom C. Clark, who had been liaison between the Justice Department and the Western Defense Command, concluded, "Looking back on it today [the evacuation] was, of course, a mistake."

Recommendations of the CWRIC (1983)

The Commission makes the following recommendations for remedies as an act of national apology.

1. That Congress pass a joint resolution, to be signed by the President, which recognizes that a grave injustice was done and offers the apologies of the nation for the acts of exclusion, removal and detention.

2. That the President pardon those who were convicted of violating the statutes imposing a curfew on American citizens. The Commission further recommends that the Department of Justice review other wartime convictions of the ethnic Japanese and recommend to the President that he pardon those whose offenses were grounded in a refusal to accept treatment that discriminated among citizens on the basis of race or ethnicity.

3. That the Congress direct the Executive agencies to which Japanese Americans may apply for the **restitution**[6] of positions, status or entitlements lost in whole or in part because of acts or events between December 1941 and 1945.

4. That the Congress demonstrate official recognition of the injustice done to American citizens of Japanese ancestry and Japanese resident aliens during the Second World War, and that it recognize the nation's need to make **redress**[7] for those events, by **appropriating**[8] monies to establish a special foundation.

The Commission believes a fund for education and humanitarian purposes related to the wartime events is appropriate and addresses an injustice suffered by an entire ethnic group.

5. The Commissioners, with the exception of Congressman Lundgren, recommended that Congress establish a fund which will provide personal redress to those who were excluded, as well as to serve the purposes set out in Recommendation #4.

Appropriations of $1.5 billion should be made to the fund over a reasonable period to be determined by

---

[6] **restitution**—the restoring of something to its rightful owner.

[7] **redress**—make amends for; to correct.

[8] **appropriating**—setting aside for a particular purpose.

Congress. The fund should be used, first, to provide a one-time per capita **compensatory**[9] payment of $20,000 to each of the approximately 60,000 surviving persons excluded from their places of residence pursuant to Executive Order 9066. The burden should be on the government to locate survivors, without requiring any application for payment, and payment should be made to the oldest survivors first. After per capita payments, the remainder of the fund should be used for the public educational purposes as discussed in Recommendation #4.

The fund should be administered by a Board, the majority of whose members are Americans of Japanese descent appointed by the President and confirmed by the Senate.

The Commission believes that, for reasons of redressing the personal injustice done to thousands of Americans and resident alien Japanese—and for compelling reasons of preserving a truthful sense of our own history and the lessons we can learn from it—these recommendations should be enacted by the Congress. In the late 1930s W. H. Auden wrote lines that express our present need to acknowledge and to make amends:

> We are left alone with our day, and time is short
> and History to the defeated
> May say Alas but cannot help or pardon

It is our belief that, though history cannot be unmade, it is well within our power to offer help, and to acknowledge error.

---

[9] **compensatory**—that which compensates for, or makes equal return for something taken.

*   *   *

After five years of delay, Congress passed and President Ronald Reagan signed, in September, 1988, a bill enacting the recommendations of the CWRIC. However, no money was appropriated to pay any of the claimants, although in late 1989 Congress scheduled payments to begin in late 1990.

QUESTIONS TO CONSIDER

1. How does examining the historical treatment of Germans and German Americans help to clarify the issue of Japanese-American internment?

2. Do you think it's appropriate for the fund to be administered by a board whose majority is of Japanese descent? Why or why not?

3. What purpose is served by including the lines from Auden's 1930s poem?

President Signs Law to Redress Wartime Wrong

THE NEW YORK TIMES, **AUGUST 11, 1988**

In 1988, following the recommendations of the Commission on Wartime Relocation and Internment of Civilians, President Reagan signed legislation which sent a personal apology to each Japanese American interned and provided for the payment of reparations to survivors. Forty-six years after internment began, the government was attempting to right some of its wrong and close an ugly chapter in American history. The following is an article from The New York Times *describing the legislation.*

Washington, Aug. 10

President Reagan, moving to "right a grave wrong," signed legislation today that apologizes for the Government's forced relocation of 120,000 Japanese Americans in World War II and establishes a $1.25

billion trust fund to pay **reparations**[1] to those who were placed in camps and to their families.

"Yes, the nation was then at war, struggling for its survival," Mr. Reagan said at the White House. "And it's not for us today to pass judgment upon those who may have made mistakes while engaged in that great struggle. Yet we must recognize that the internment of Japanese Americans was just that, a mistake."

Under the law, the Government will issue individual apologies for all violations of civil liberties and constitutional rights. And, through the office of the United States Attorney General, an award of $20,000 in tax-free payments will be given to each eligible intern or the designated **beneficiary**[2] of the approximately 60,000 surviving Japanese Americans who were driven from their homes and placed in internment camps in the war. Legislation providing the money must still be enacted.

Veto[3] Had Been Threatened

Mr. Reagan had threatened to veto the measure but went ahead and signed it today. The White House spokesman, Marlin Fitzwater, said that the president had been concerned about the price tag of the bill, not its concept. In signing the legislation, Mr. Reagan endorsed the position that Vice President Bush staked out in June on the eve of the California primary.

About 40 percent of those affected by the legislation live in California, according to Congressional estimates.

The While House denied, as it has frequently done in recent weeks, that Mr. Reagan's initial opposition to the measure was reversed in part to help Mr. Bush in California.

When asked whether Mr. Bush's electoral prospects were responsible for Mr. Reagan's change of heart,

---

[1] **reparations**—reimbursements; compensations for damage.

[2] **beneficiary**—a recipient of benefits.

[3] **Veto**—to reject, deny, or refuse.

Mr. Fitzwater replied, "No, they were not a factor in any way."

Congressional aides who are familiar with the bill's history said today, however, that there had been some pressure on the White House to sign the bill, particularly from California Republicans. But Democratic aides questioned whether such lobbying carried more weight than the bill's merits.

"There were a lot of contacts to the White House at various levels from a lot of different people," said an aide to a Democratic Congressman from California. "It's an important piece of legislation. I have to believe that all of the forces were working on this. They have made it possible."

Internment Ordered In 1942

Japanese Americans were interned as a result of an executive order by President Roosevelt in 1942. About 77,000 American citizens and 43,000 legal and illegal resident aliens were affected by the order. The last camp was closed in January 1946, five months after World War II ended.

Mr. Fitzwater said that reparations will be extended to any person of Japanese ancestry who was a United States citizen or "permanent resident alien" living in the United States during the "relocation period" from Dec. 7, 1941, to June 30, 1946.

That includes individuals who were confined, held in custody, relocated or "otherwise deprived of liberty as a result of specific actions of the Federal government during the war," he said. The payments will begin in about one year and will be spread over a 10-year period with priority given to the elderly.

The bill also provides compensation of $12,000 to each of the surviving wartime evacuees from the Aleutian and Pribilof Islands in Alaska.

Annual Appropriation Limited

No more than $500 million will be appropriated annually, Mr. Fitzwater added. And, in accepting the money, internees must agree to drop all legal claims pending against the Government.

Mark Sheehan, a spokesman for the Justice Department, said there is one case now pending, *Hohri v. U.S.* Lower courts had ruled that the case should be dismissed, in part because the statute of limitations had run out. The plaintiffs now have a short time remaining to ask the Supreme Court to hear the case, he said.

Mr. Reagan, in his remarks in the Old Executive Office Building to 200 Japanese Americans and Congressional supporters of the bill, took special note of the "scores of Japanese Americans" who volunteered to serve in the United States armed forces in the war.

"The 442nd Regimental Combat Team, made up entirely of Japanese Americans served with immense distinction to defend this nation, their nation," the President said. "Yet back at home, the soldiers' families were being denied the very freedom for which so many of the soldiers themselves were laying down their lives."

Congressmen in Audience

Among those listening in the audience were Representative Norman Y. Mineta, Democrat of California and the sponsor of the House-passed reparations bill; Senator Spark M. Matsunaga, Democrat of Hawaii and the bill's chief Senate sponsor; and Senator Daniel K. Inouye, the Hawaii Democrat, who served in the 442nd regiment and lost his right arm fighting in Italy. He was awarded a Bronze Star and two Purple Hearts.

All three men are of Japanese descent. Mr. Mineta, as a 10-year-old child, was interned with his family during the war, first in converted stables and barracks at the Santa Anita race track in California. Later, over the period of three years during which he was interned, he was moved from California to Heart Mountain, Wyo.

Senator Matsunaga, who was wounded twice in the war after participating in the Anzio landing in Italy, was also detained with other Japanese Americans at Camp McCoy, Wis., after the attack on Pearl Harbor. At the time, he was a second lieutenant and a company commander in the Army.

"No payment can make up for those lost years," Mr. Reagan said. "What is most important in this bill has less to do with property than with honor. For here we admit wrong."

QUESTIONS TO CONSIDER

1. Based on the information provided, do you think President Reagan's decision to sign the bill was motivated by political pressure? Explain your response.

2. In exchange for the compensation it offered, what did the U.S. government expect from the internees? Do you think it's a reasonable expectation?

3. Do you believe that "justice delayed is justice denied," or is it possible to restore justice despite a long delay? Support your answer.

ACKNOWLEDGEMENTS

10 from *Eagle Against the Sun: The American War with Japan* by Ronald H. Spector. Reprinted with the permission of The Free Press, a Division of Simon & Schuster, Inc. Copyright ©1984 by Ronald H. Spector.

30 "The Stranger Within Our Gates," *Time,* January 19, 1942. ©1942 Time Inc. Reprinted by permission.

31 "Today and Tomorrow—The Fifth Column on the Coast" by Walter Lippmann in *New York Herald Tribune,* Feb. 12, 1942. Copyright 1942 by the New York Times Co. Reprinted by permission.

46 "Apes and Others" from *War Without Mercy* by John W. Dower. Copyright © 1986 by John W. Dower. Reprinted by permission of Pantheon Books, a division of Random House, Inc.

56 "A Birthright Renounced: Joseph Kurihara," from Joseph Kurihara, autobiography, typescript, in Japanese Evacuation and Relocation Study, call number: 67/14C, box no. A17.05, pp. 1-52, Bancroft Library, University of California, Berkeley.

85 From *Desert Exile: The Uprooting of a Japanese American Family* by Yoshiko Uchida (University of Washington Press, 1982). Courtesy of the Bancroft Library, University of California, Berkeley.

101 Excerpt from *Snow Falling on Cedars,* copyright © 1994 by David Guterson, reprinted by permission of Harcourt Brace & Company.

111 "In Response to Executive Order 9066" is from *Crossing with the Light* by Dwight Okita (Tia Chucha Press). Used by permission of author.

112 "Warning"" by Mitsuye Yamada, in *Making More Waves* ed. by Elaine H. Kim et al. Boston: Beacon Press, 1997. Reprinted by permission of Mitsuye Yamada.

124 From *Nisei Daughter* by Monica Sone. Copyright ©1953 by Monica Sone; © renewed 1981 by Monica Sone. By permission of Little, Brown and Company.

134 From *Citizen 13660* by Miné Okubo. Reprinted with permission from Deborah Gesensway and Mindy Roseman, *Beyond Words: Images from America's Concentration Camps* (Ithaca, NY: Cornell University Press, 1987), pp. 66-74.

142 From *Lone Heart Mountain* by Estelle Ishigo, (Los Angeles, 1972), pp. 55-72.

149 Images from Estelle Ishigo, Lone Heart Mountain (Los Angeles, 1972), pp. 1, 6, 32, 76.

155 "Shikata Ga Nai" reprinted from *The Winters of That Country: Tales of the Man-Made Seasons* with the permission of Black Sparrow Press. Copyright © 1984 by John Sanford.

159 "That Damned Fence" by Anonymous, Japanese American Relocation Center Records. Division of Rare and Manuscript Collections, Cornell University Library.

160 "My Mom, Pop, and Me" by Itsuko Taniguchi, Japanese American Relocation Center Records. Division of Rare and Manuscript Collections, Cornell University Library.

161 "Manzanar" by Michiko Mizumoto, Japanese American Relocation Center Records. Division of Rare and Manuscript Collections, Cornell University Library.

205 "Breaking Silence" by Janice Mirikitani. Copyright © 1995 by Janice Mirikitani. From *We, the Dangerous* by Janice Mirikitani, Celestial Arts Publisher, Berkeley, CA, 1995. Reprinted by permission of the author.

208 "In Remembrance" by Janice Mirikitani. From *Making Waves* edited by Asian Women United of California. © 1989 by Asian Women United of California. Reprinted by permission of Beacon Press, Boston.

211 "When We Were Children" by Richard Oyama. Transfer 38, ed. Paul Bailiff (San Francisco: Community Press, 1979), p. 43.

213 From *Farewell to Manzanar* by James D. and Jeanne Wakatsuki Houston. Copyright © 1973 by James D. Houston. Reprinted by permission of Houghton Mifflin Co. All rights reserved.

232 "President Signs Law to Redress Wartime Wrong," *The New York Times,* national edition, August 11, 1988, A16. Copyright © 1988 by the New York Times Co. Reprinted by permission.

Photo Research Diane Hamilton

Photos Courtesy of the Library of Congress and the National Archives.

Every effort has been made to secure complete rights and permissions for each selection presented herein. Updated acknowledgements, if needed, will appear in subsequent printings.

Index